Resilience God Style

Study Guide

Major General Bob Dees
US Army, Retired

www.ResilienceGodStyle.com

Creative Team Publishing
Ft. Worth, TX

© 2018 by Robert F. Dees.

All rights reserved. No part of this study guide may be reproduced, stored in a retrieval system or transmitted in any form or by any means without the prior written permission of the publisher, except by a reviewer who may quote brief passages in a review to be distributed through electronic media, or printed in a newspaper, magazine or journal.

SCRIPTURE REFERENCES:

All scripture quotations, unless otherwise indicated, are taken from the New American Standard Bible, Copyright © 1960, 1962, 1963, 1968, 1971, 1972, 1973, 1975, 1977, 1995 by The Lockman Foundation. Used by permission. (http://www.Lockman.org)

Scripture quotations marked "NKJV™" are taken from the New King James Version. Copyright © 1982 by Thomas Nelson, Inc. Used by permission. All rights reserved.

Scripture quotations marked (NIV) are taken from the Holy Bible, New International Version®, NIV®. Copyright © 1973, 1978, 1984, 2011 by Biblica, Inc.™ Used by permission of Zondervan. All rights reserved worldwide. http://www.zondervan.com. The "NIV" and "New International Version" are trademarks registered in the United States Patent and Trademark Office by Biblica, Inc.™

Scripture quotations marked (NLT) are taken from the Holy Bible, New Living Translation, copyright © 1996, 2004, 2007. Used by permission of Tyndale House Publishers, Inc., Carol Stream, Illinois 60188. All rights reserved.

PERMISSIONS AND CREDITS:

Grateful acknowledgment is made to the following for permission to cite previously published material, quotes and concepts: Excerpts from *Resilience God Style*, © 2018 Robert F. Dees, used with permission of Robert F. Dees, Resilience Consulting LLC. All rights reserved.

DISCLAIMERS:

This study guide is not a substitute for appropriate medical or psychological care for those experiencing significant emotional pain or whose ability to function at home, school, or work is impaired. Chronic or extreme stress may cause a wide assortment of physical and psychological problems. Some may require evaluation and treatment by medical or mental health professionals. When in doubt, seek advice from a professional. You must not rely on the information in this study guide as an alternative to medical advice from your doctor or other professional healthcare provider. If you have any specific questions about any medical matter you should consult your doctor or other professional healthcare provider. If you think you may be suffering from any medical condition you should seek immediate medical attention. You should never delay seeking medical advice, disregard medical advice, or discontinue medical treatment because of information in this study guide.

During the process of constructing this study guide, due diligence has been undertaken to obtain all proper copyright permissions. If it comes to our attention that any citations are missing, they will be readily provided at http://www.ResilienceGodStyle.com.

ISBN: 978-0-9979519-3-6
PUBLISHED BY CREATIVE TEAM PUBLISHING
www.CreativeTeamPublishing.com
Ft. Worth, Texas
Printed in the United States of America

Resilience God Style Study Guide

Major General Bob Dees

US Army, Retired

www.ResilienceGodStyle.com

Table of Contents

Purpose and Use		9
Resilience Life Cycle© Diagram		13
1	Incoming!	15
	Incoming in Your Life?	15
	Evil Is Real	17
	Tribulation Is Real	19
	God Is Real	19
	Regaining Altitude	22
2	Trauma	25
	Defining Trauma	25
	Avoiding the Misconceptions of Trauma	26
	Regaining Altitude	29
3	Growth	31
	Posttraumatic Growth (PTG)	31
	Posttraumatic Growth in Action: Joseph	32
	Hope or Bitterness	34
	Regaining Altitude	35
4	Resilience Life Cycle©	37
	"Resilience Life Cycle©" Diagram	37
	Before	39
	During	40
	After	41

Table of Contents

	Tennis Ball or Egg?	44
	Regaining Altitude	47
5	BEFORE: Building Bounce—The Ounce of Prevention	49
	Know Your Calling (Mission, Purpose)	49
	Know Your Enemy (Vulnerabilities, Threats)	50
	Know Your Friends	51
	Know Your Equipment (Armor of God)	52
	Consistent and Comprehensive Prayer (Chart)	55
	Deploy with the Right Mindset	55
	Develop and Rehearse "Actions on Contact" (Get Ready!)	56
	Regaining Altitude	57
6	DURING: Weathering the Storm	59
	Call 911 (Ask for Help)	59
	Start the IV (Nurture Yourself)	62
	Keep Breathing (Maintain Routines)	64
	Draw from Your Well of Courage (Past Experiences)	68
	Remember Your Calling	70
	Regaining Altitude	71
7	AFTER: Bouncing Back...Without Getting Stuck!	73
	Guard Your Primary Relationships	73
	Choose Forgiveness and Gratitude	76
	Grieve Well	78
	Regaining Altitude	80
8	AFTER: Bouncing Ahead...Into a Hopeful Future	81
	Sing a New Song	81
	Revalidate Your Calling (Discern and Chart the Future)	83
	Comfort Others	87
	Regaining Altitude	89

Table of Contents

9	LEARN AND ADAPT: Getting Ready...Again!	91
	Learn and Adapt Observations:	91
	Know Your Calling	91
	Know Your Enemy	92
	Know Your Friends	92
	Know Your Equipment	93
	Deploy with Right Mindset	93
	Actions on Contact	94
	If I Could Do It Over	94
	Being A Lifetime Learner	95
	Growth Through Adversity Tool	96
	Regaining Altitude	96
10	LEARN AND ADAPT: And Even Higher!	97
	The Ultimate Resilient Warrior—Jesus Christ	97
	Regaining Altitude	99

About the Author	101
Bibliography	105
Appendix 1: Products and Services	113
Appendix 2: Resilience Life Cycle© Summary Diagram	115
Appendix 3: Growth Through Adversity Diagram	117
Appendix 4: Fleeing a Spirit of Offense	119

Purpose and Use

Resilience God Style Study Guide

Were you in actual military combat today (and you may be), you would be highly focused on preparing for the next fight, doing everything possible to stay alive and accomplish your mission. While not diminishing the unique experiences of warriors engaged in military conflict, the reality is <u>all of us are in combat</u>, we are all "at war." Your battles may be different from mine, but <u>we are all warriors</u>. As warriors, we fight… we get wounded (suffering), we bounce back (resilience), and we fight again (reengagement). That is the human condition in a fallen world.

> We are all "at war."

However ferocious or tame our current battles are, none of us can predict the intensity of our future life battles, the depth of our wounds, or the height of our resilient strength or joy. <u>We do know, however, that training and preparation lead to Comprehensive Personal Fitness™, a full-spectrum readiness that will maximize our potential to survive the rigors of war, be they physical, mental, spiritual, emotional, or relational</u>.

This *Resilience God Style Study Guide* will guide your application of *Resilience God Style* precepts and practices in order to achieve this readiness, particularly the spiritual readiness, which the battles of life require.

The Book of James in the New Testament states:

"But prove yourselves <u>doers of the word</u>, and not merely hearers who delude themselves. <u>For if anyone is a hearer of the word and not a doer</u>, he is like a man who looks at his natural face in a mirror; for once he has looked at himself and gone away, <u>he has immediately forgotten what kind of person he was</u>. But one who <u>looks intently at the perfect law</u>, the law of liberty, <u>and abides by it</u>, not having become a forgetful hearer but an effectual doer, <u>this man will be blessed in what he does</u>." (James 1: 22-25, underline emphasis added)

This *Resilience God Style Study Guide* is <u>your tool</u> to accomplish the above. From my own life experience, I can testify that I have not always been a good steward of the knowledge and life experiences God has brought my way. Time and again I have seen that knowledge and experience become useful only when they are properly integrated into the context of my life; in essence, personalized. Such <u>personalized application of knowledge</u> is essential to attaining true wisdom and avoiding the pitfalls of staying "on the sidelines" as a hearer, but not a doer.

This *Resilience God Style Study Guide* is simple in concept, but potentially life changing. It provides "processes" by which you can reflect and record your specific attitudes, applications, and actions as you allow God to transform you from the inside out.

Further dissecting the principles set forth in *Resilience God Style*, this study guide will help you consolidate your perspectives about the reality and the role of tribulation, trauma, and suffering. As well, this study guide will assist you in the BEFORE-DURING-AFTER-LEARN AND ADAPT phases of responding to trial and tribulation, trauma and tragedy, <u>in your life</u> as an individual warrior, or possibly as a leader or a caregiver. <u>The real power here is derived not from the answers but from the questions which usher us into personal considerations and applications</u>. The blank spaces provide golden opportunities for you to get beyond simple hearing, to authentic and effective thinking and doing, processes which best equip you to deal with your battles of the past, present, and future as a resilient warrior.

You can complete this guided study individually, but it is much better if you have a battle buddy. Hold one another accountable for completing and following your personal observations and commitments in your battle book.

In like manner, use this study guide in a small group setting and tap the power of community and teamwork in bringing about true-life change for you and for others. Whether used alone or with others, make this study guide your personal, comprehensive tool to help you prepare for and navigate the "cleverly disguised opportunities," the body slams of life that will most certainly come your way.

One other recommendation before you begin: start where you are. You may be in the middle of <u>a huge, debilitating storm of life right now</u>. If so, after gaining empathy and context from Chapters 1 - 3 in *Resilience God Style*, I suggest you dive into Chapter 6, "Weathering the Storm". This may be where you are experientially and emotionally at present. God will meet you there with His compassion, comfort, and counsel.

Perhaps you are <u>in the middle of bouncing back</u> from a tragic experience, a reversal, a deep pain and hurt that seems to go on and on. After "water skiing" through *Resilience God Style* and the *Resilience God Style Study Guide* to gain context, I suggest you "scuba dive" into Chapters 6 - 8 as a first focus of study and application. God will also meet you there.

Finally, it may be that <u>the sun is shining brightly for you now</u>, you sense the wind at your back, and your well of courage is brimming with optimism and expectation regarding a bright and hopeful future. <u>Or you may sense storm clouds on the horizon</u> and do not want to be caught off guard. <u>For you the simply admonition is, "Get Ready."</u> Now is the time to prepare well for the next hurricane or tornado in your life. God will meet you in this time of preparation, allowing you to "learn and adapt" from previous life experiences, to "build bounce," to develop a resilience that will sustain you and others in the coming days.

To help you keep the "big picture" in mind, note the Resilience Life Cycle© Summary Diagram on page 13, with the specific "Before", "During", and "After" categories. (Also see *Resilience God Style*, page 223). For your convenience and frequent referral, this diagram is also contained as Appendix 2 in this study guide. Also for your convenience, we have left significant space in this *Study Guide* for subsequent reflections over time as future life challenges reveal new wisdom and practical means for growth. Your personal observations and related biblical precepts will become "nuggets of gold" and "rivers of living water" in your future dark moments of life. <u>Compile, store, and guard them for later use</u>.

As a final charge, I challenge you to <u>make the most of this opportunity</u>. I'm sure I have read (or at least started) thousands of books over my lifetime, but the reality is that a much smaller number (in the tens) have truly impacted and changed my life for the better. The selections in this smaller category have become my "best friends." I visit them repeatedly and dissect them often, recognizing that new *knowledge* is not nearly as important as new (and renewed) *applications* of bedrock truth that have proven enduring and effective.

While knowledge across a broad range of topics is useful, <u>mastery of a small number of essential life skills is critical to survival when the strong winds blow in your life</u>. Bouncing back is one of those essential life skills.

My prayer is that this *Resilience God Style Study Guide* will become a valuable tool to help you achieve the mastery you need to truly maximize your potential as a resilient warrior.

Let's dive in!

> While knowledge across a broad range of topics is useful,
> <u>mastery of a small number of essential life skills is critical to survival</u>
> <u>when the strong winds blow in your life</u>.

RESILIENCE LIFE CYCLE©

LEARN & ADAPT

Building Resilience | Weathering the Storm | Bouncing Back

Before — **During** — **After**

Source: *Resilience God Style,* page 78

Before

- Know Your Calling (Mission, Purpose)
- Know Your Enemy
- Know Your Friends
- Know Your Equipment (Armor of God)
- Deploy with the Right Mindset
- Develop and Rehearse "Actions on Contact" (Get Ready!)

During

- Call 911 (Ask for help)
- Start the IV (Nurture yourself)
- Keep Breathing (Maintain routines)
- Draw from Your Well of Courage (Past strengths)
- Remember Your Calling

After

- Guard Your Primary Relationships
- Choose Forgiveness and Gratitude
- Grieve Well
- Sing a New Song
- Revalidate Your Calling (Discern and Chart the Future)
- Comfort Others

1
INCOMING!

(See *Resilience God Style*, Chapter 1)

> "We are all at war, whether on the battlefront or the home front, whether in the board room or the class room. War is a reality for each of us. We all take incoming."
> (*Resilience God Style*, Chapter 1, page 39)

INCOMING IN YOUR LIFE?

A. **What does "incoming" look like in your life?** Name the three most recent life experiences when you truly felt "body slammed."

1) _____
_____
_____
_____
_____
_____
_____

2) _____
_____
_____
_____
_____
_____

3) _____

B. **How did you "feel" when these experiences (above) occurred? What common denominators existed across all these life challenges?** (Fear? Inability to control? Anger? Other?)

C. **How would you define "tribulation?"**

D. **What is the likelihood that you will experience tribulation in the future? Why?**

_____
_____
_____
_____
_____
_____
_____

EVIL IS REAL

"Evil is a reality <u>in our world</u>, it also comes packaged <u>in our own sinfulness</u>, and it supernaturally appears <u>in the form of fallen angelic beings</u> who wage war against our souls. Evil results in tribulation. This is real for each of us, and it hurts." (*Resilience God Style*, page 43)

E. **What personal life experiences or observations convince you regarding the existence of evil?** Examine each source of evil:

1) The Natural World (other people, natural disasters)

_____
_____
_____
_____
_____
_____

2) The Human World (our own sinfulness)

_____
_____
_____

3) The Spirit World (unseen spiritual forces)

F. **Do you have a personal example where you have "looked evil in the face?"**

TRIBULATION IS REAL

Tribulation is the logical consequence of evil in our world. We see it all around us. While tribulation often happens "to the other guy," it becomes more than a concept when it happens to us:

"Tribulation is often defined more personally, however. Perhaps it's the loss of <u>your</u> house, <u>your</u> job, or <u>your</u> closest loved one. Perhaps it's the privation of <u>your</u> health, or <u>your</u> life's work, or <u>your</u> reputation. Perhaps it's a crisis of faith, or a "dark night of the soul." Perhaps it's the total devastation of natural disasters: earthquakes, tsunamis, hurricanes, tornadoes, flooding, or fires. The list is endless." (*Resilience God Style*, page 46)

G. **How has tribulation impacted you personally? Consistent with the definitions of tribulation, did you feel like you were being "squeezed?" Did you feel like the tribulation served to separate the wheat from the chaff in your life?** (For example, did you find that family became more important to you, while possessions and money became less important?)

_____
_____
_____
_____
_____
_____
_____
_____
_____
_____
_____
_____

GOD IS REAL

"Most of us in the real world do not question the reality of evil, sin, suffering, and tribulation. Many, however, do <u>question the existence of God or His good character</u>. Common reasoning goes like this: "God, if You are good and loving, if You created this earth, then why is there so much pain? <u>Why is there suffering in this world</u>? And, in particular, God, why does it have to come down on me? I am a good person. What have I done wrong? <u>I don't deserve this</u>!" (*Resilience God Style*, page 47, underline emphasis added)

H. **In light of the presence of evil and the resulting tribulation in this world, do you ever question the existence of God, His good character, or His care for you, and how do you express your doubt or disbelief?**

_____
_____
_____
_____
_____
_____
_____

I. **Do you also question, "Why is there suffering in this world?" or more personally, "Why do *I* have to suffer?"** [Note: for a more theological approach, consider the "theology of suffering." Said another way: In God's economy is there "logic" behind suffering?) **Informed by your** *Resilience God Style* **reading or other life observations, explain your thoughts about these fundamental questions.**

_____
_____
_____
_____
_____
_____
_____

J. **Reflect upon a past experience when you clearly observed that "God is real."** (Reference page 47, *Resilience God Style*)

_____
_____
_____
_____
_____
_____
_____
_____
_____
_____

K. Finally, let's not close without providing an "earnest payment" which reminds us that despite the reality of evil, pain, suffering, trial, and tribulation, we are more than conquerors through Him who love us. **Specifically, consider some bedrock verses which provide hope and optimism for the future. Summarize what these mean to you in the spaces below; discuss them with your battle buddy or small group.**

    1) Psalm 34:18

_____
_____
_____
_____

    2) Hebrews 6:18,19

_____
_____
_____
_____

3) Romans 8:37-39

_____
_____
_____
_____

4) 1 Thessalonians 4:13,14

_____
_____
_____
_____

5) 1 John 4:4

_____
_____
_____
_____

REGAINING ALTITUDE

With height comes perspective. Let us "gain altitude" as we close out this first study chapter. Although it is important for us to begin a discussion of resilience with the existence of evil in our world and the reality of trial and tribulation, pain, and suffering, we won't camp here for very long. Psalm 130:6 says, "My soul waits for the Lord more than the watchmen for the morning; Indeed, more than the watchmen for the morning." As well, we all understand the principle that "light shines best in darkness."

Hence, I encourage you to "hang in there" while we lay important foundations. Hang in there while we deal with the reality of darkness in the world and pain in our own lives. I know that this can be very difficult work, usually best accomplished with your battle buddy and with the comfort and counsel of the Holy Spirit.

After these important preliminaries which delve into personal specifics of pain and trauma, you and I will even better appreciate the sharp contrast of bright new vistas, broadened perspectives, and greater resilience that God is building into our lives. As you continue to wrestle with questions which basically revolve around "What does all this mean to me?" I exhort you to courageously press forward.

You can do it!

> "These things I have spoken to you, that in <u>Me</u> you may have peace.
> In the world you will have tribulation, but be of good cheer, <u>I have overcome the world</u>."
> (John 16:33, NKJV, underline emphasis added)

2
Trauma

(See *Resilience God Style*, Chapter 2)

> "In the blink of an eye, he experiences something that will haunt him for a lifetime. He did not intend this; it runs counter to everything he stands for, it makes him want to vomit, it generates false guilt for something out of his control, it causes him to question the nobility of his cause, it makes him want to quit." (*Resilience God Style*, page 52, describing Jacob Callaway's "moral wound" from combat in Afghanistan)

DEFINING TRAUMA

Trauma comes packaged in different ways: sometimes totally by surprise, sometimes with an agonizing knowledge of impending doom. It comes sometimes at the hand of an enemy, and sometimes at the hand of a friend. Some trauma is physically observable: a cut, a broken bone, a deep bruise. Some trauma is not seen, held captive in the heart, the soul, the spirit, and the mind of the grief bearer.

A. **Based upon your own life experiences and *Resilience God Style* definitions, how would you define trauma?**

_____
_____
_____
_____

_____
_____

B. **Why is it useful to think about trauma before it occurs to you?**

_____
_____
_____
_____
_____
_____
_____
_____
_____

AVOIDING THE MISCONCEPTIONS OF TRAUMA

"Many a well-meaning person has further wounded a trauma sufferer by implying that sin or wrong doing were the reason for someone's inexplicable tragedy. Although there are times when God brings discipline into our lives and wrongdoing carries consequences which are painful; pain, tragedy, trauma, and tribulation are not punishments from God." (*Resilience God Style*, page 57)

C. **As with the disciples' assessment of the blind man in John, Chapter 9, have you sometimes concluded that pain, tragedy, trauma, and tribulation are personal punishments from God for sinful actions?**

_____

1) **Is this conclusion logical or consistent with biblical truth? Provide justification for your answer.**

_____
_____
_____

2) **What modern day <u>counterexamples</u> come to mind?** (For example, a wounded soldier doing "a good work" in combat in order to save the lives of others. His wounds and the ensuing trauma are clearly <u>not</u> the result of his own sin. This is <u>not</u> a personal punishment from God.)

D. **Is pain productive?**

1) **Identify an example from your own life.** (To guide your thoughts, consider some of the traumatic life experiences that you cited in Chapter 1 of this study guide. Which of those have resulted in growth? Which of those might still possess "growth spurt potential" as you process them in the context of *Resilience God Style*?)

_____

_____

If you have successfully identified a painful experience that resulted in personal growth, pause right now to thank God. Pray as well that you will have the perspective to reflexively "count it all joy" in future trials of life.

Record your prayer here.

_____
_____
_____
_____
_____
_____
_____
_____
_____
_____

2) **Identify an example from someone else's life as a way to further solidify the principle that "gain most often comes from pain."** (We can often more easily observe this principle at work in someone else's life: a child, an employee, a family member, or a close friend).

_____
_____
_____
_____
_____
_____
_____

3) Using the other misconceptions about pain, trauma and suffering contained on **pages 51-53** of *Resilience God Style*, **identify where you (or others you have observed) viewed pain through an improper lens** (unproductive, indicates spiritual failure, will not lead to good, or incompatible with the basic nature of a good and loving God).

_____
_____
_____
_____
_____
_____
_____
_____

REGAINING ALTITUDE

"Let's gain altitude. With height comes perspective. It is now clear. In the world we have tribulation. You and I simply need to listen to today's news, or remember the body slams of dear family and friends, or think about Job's suffering, or Jacob in Afghanistan, or reflect on our own life experiences and we are convinced.

"Trauma results from such tribulation. When trauma is misinterpreted it leads to wrong responses and false conclusions about the role of pain and suffering in our lives, as well as the role God plays through our pain and suffering. Trauma is real and we really need to understand it in order to be resilient through it.

"Humpty Dumpty did sit on a wall, and he did have a great fall. How do we mend the broken pieces, how do we properly respond to trauma, how do we bounce back, or even better, how do we bounce to higher levels of personal and professional fulfillment than ever before?" (*Resilience God Style*, page 59, underline emphasis added)

Having wrestled with the realities of pain and suffering, we now turn the corner to establish a spiritual resilience framework in our lives.

> Consider it all joy, my brethren, when you encounter various trials, knowing that the testing of your faith produces endurance. And let endurance have *its* perfect result, so that you may be perfect and complete, lacking in nothing. (James 1:2-4)

3
Growth

(See *Resilience God Style*, Chapter 3)

> Bitter or better? That is the question. Because tribulation is real and trauma is inevitable, we must consider our reactions. "How will we respond to the curve balls of life?" is a real question. "Do we get bitter or better?" (*Resilience God Style*, page 63)

POSTTRAUMATIC GROWTH (PTG)

The concept of PTG is a useful launch point as we seek to build bounce, as we pursue resilience. (*Resilience God Style*, page 62)

A. **Summarize what posttraumatic growth (PTG) means to you. If possible, draw a picture of what PTG looks like:**

_____
_____
_____
_____
_____
_____
_____

Picture:

POSTTRAUMATIC GROWTH (PTG) IN ACTION: JOSEPH

"If anyone possessed opportunities to grow bitter, to strike back, to get even with his betrayers, his accusers, his captors, he did! Yet, this man was <u>able to grow through adversity</u> into an arena of self-actualization and contribution that he or others would have never anticipated or predicted." (*Resilience God Style*, page 74, describing Joseph's journey from tribulation to growth and transformation, underline emphasis added)

B. *Joseph is certainly a great example from the scriptures regarding posttraumatic growth.* **Who else from the pages of scripture illustrates growth after trauma? Describe their journeys below:**

_____
_____
_____
_____
_____
_____
_____
_____
_____

C. In a similar fashion, there are many real world examples of posttraumatic growth (Joni Erickson Tada, Congresswoman Gabi Giffords, Captain Scott Smiley, U.S. Army, et al). **Describe how you or someone you have observed has grown stronger and more resilient despite (and because of) the trauma they have faced:**

_____
_____
_____
_____
_____
_____
_____
_____
_____

D. Often the negative example of someone also instructs us. As mentioned, the scriptures reflect people whose stories are just like ours. **Can you think of an example from the Bible of one who got bitter and not necessarily better? What do we learn from this?** (If an example doesn't come to mind, consider the Prophet Jonah. While the book of Jonah does illustrate positive themes of repentance and forgiveness, the Prophet Jonah was often inclined to anger and bitterness, essentially reduced to "pouting" when the city of Nineveh repented. See Jonah, Chapter 4.)

_____
_____
_____
_____
_____
_____
_____
_____

HOPE OR BITTERNESS?

"Whether you are a young wounded warrior whose future has been changed forever, or a businessman whose life's work has been negated by a sudden reversal, or a senior citizen facing mortality in the twilight of your life, this spiritual dynamic is essential. <u>Through spiritual engagement and growth we all can prosper in hope, avoiding the debilitating shackles of bitterness, growing through adversity.</u> This is the "secret sauce" of resilience which will be discussed at greater lengths in forthcoming chapters." (*Resilience God Style*, page 75, underlined emphasis added)

E. Reflect upon the profound quotation by Dr Jerry White on page 65 of *Resilience God Style*. As Dr White suggests, spiritual growth makes the difference between outcomes of hope and bitterness. **Have you observed this principle in action in your life, or in the lives of others? How do you insure that you make the right choices toward spiritual growth that lead to growth and not bitterness?**

_____
_____
_____
_____
_____
_____
_____

F. By this time, the "Bounce Builders" in *Resilience God Style* should have gotten your attention (at end of Chapter 2 and forward). In this vein, many of the great movies of our day are based upon stories that show how underdogs fight through adversity to become better and not bitter, often making a significant impact on others in the process. **What such movie comes to mind for you? Why did it move your spirit so powerfully?**

_____
_____
_____

_____

_____

_____

_____

REGAINING ALTITUDE

"This story could just as easily been lifted from the headlines of today's paper: betrayal, violence, trauma, <u>a choice between bitter or better, and the outcomes of anger and desperation, or growth and fulfillment</u>. Joseph took the fork in the road towards growth. That's the one I want." (*Resilience God Style*, page 74, underline emphasis added)

Over my entire adult life, I have encountered many who were trapped by bitterness, perhaps for days or for decades. We will deal specifically with how to flee bitterness in later chapters, but at this point we should recognize that this is one of the primary "landmines" that will derail us from growth through trauma. Bitterness becomes like a cancer, eating away our outward physical vitality and eroding our emotional, relational, and spiritual strength, optimism, and resilience.

The simple question of "better or bitter?" is one of the most fundamental issues of life, for all of us. We now move forward to growth and resilience.

> Therefore, since we have so great a cloud of witnesses surrounding us, <u>let us also lay aside every encumbrance and the sin which so easily entangles us</u>, and <u>let us run with endurance the race that is set before us</u>, fixing our eyes on Jesus, the author and perfecter of faith, who <u>for the joy set before Him endured the cross</u>, despising the shame, and has sat down at the right hand of the throne of God. For consider Him who has endured such hostility by sinners against Himself, <u>so that you will not grow weary and lose heart</u>.
> (Hebrews 12:1-3, highlighting Jesus as one who stayed the course and did not succumb to bitterness, underline emphasis added)

4
Resilience Life Cycle ©

(See *Resilience God Style*, Chapter 4)

RESILIENCE LIFE CYCLE©

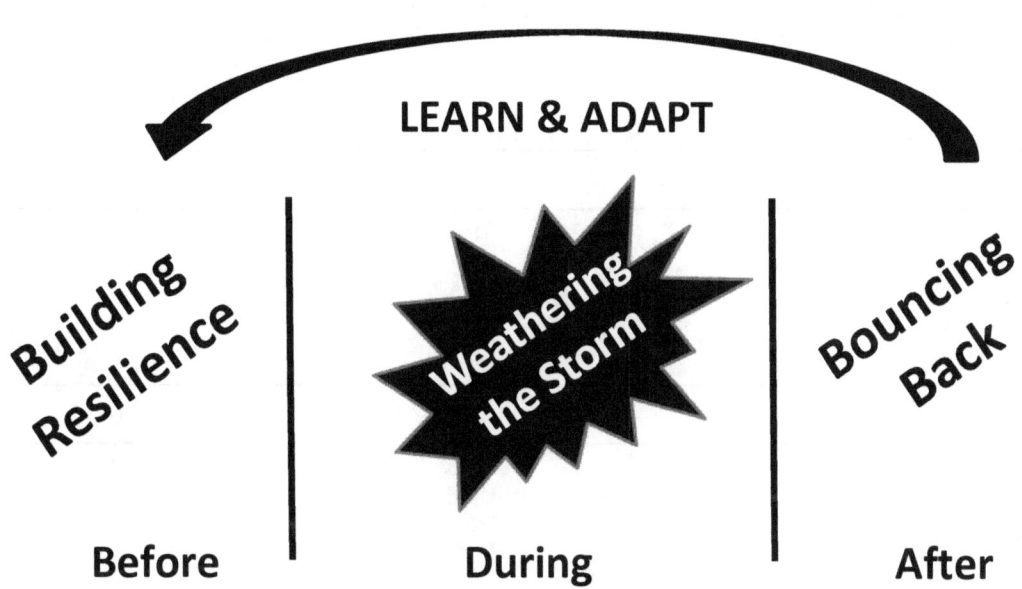

Source: *Resilience God Style,* page 78

Chapter 4 sets forth the Resilience Life Cycle© model before we expand upon each component in the remainder of *Resilience God Style*. Hence, this is an opportune time to do some <u>self-assessment</u> before we dive into the specifics.

The story of U.S. Army Captain Scott Smiley and his wife Tiffany provides an inspiring golden thread for this chapter, depicting their Before, During, and After experiences surrounding the life changing events which they faced. In like fashion, each of us can look at our own responses to a past trauma. The questions below will help each of us look at a past trauma through new eyes. Note that Appendix 3 includes a diagram that graphically summarizes these Before-During-After questions.

A. First, **restate here <u>one</u> of your life traumas** that you identified in Chapters 1 or 2 of this *Resilience God Style Study Guide*. State it below in Who? What? Where? When? fashion, recognizing that you may still not have Why? figured out:

WHO?
_____
_____

WHAT?
_____
_____

WHERE?
_____
_____

WHEN?
_____
_____

Now we will step through each phase of the Resilience Life Cycle© to conduct our self-assessment. Do your best answering the questions, and be willing to share openly with your battle buddy (or others). Although you don't yet have full benefit of the precepts and practices that will come to light later in our study together, your sincere effort to conduct this preliminary self-assessment will make your subsequent learning more productive.

BEFORE

"We are warriors, all of us. As warriors, we must be prepared. We can build bounce and increase resilience ahead of time before encountering the next tribulation and trauma that are sure to come. This is the preventive phase and we all must consider and act upon it." (*Resilience God Style,* page 79, underline emphasis added)

B. As you reflect back to the traumatic experience which you laid out in "A" above, **do you feel you were "well prepared" for this body slam?**

_____
_____
_____
_____
_____
_____
_____

C. If you knew that a similar trauma would soon happen again, **name five (5) actions you can take to "get ready" for this coming storm?**

1) _____

2) _____

3) _____

4) _____

5) _____

DURING

"God truly allowed them and others who walked with them, to *weather the storm* with grace and full confidence that God was going through the storm with them. While waves of remorse and doubt understandably roll through periodically, this couple has consistently been remarkably, and some would term miraculously, positive and productive." (*Resilience God Style*, page 81, referring to how Scott and Tiffany Smiley "weathered the storm")

D. Continuing to reflect upon the traumatic event you have described in "A" above, **assess how you "weathered the storm."** If you are married, also assess how you and your spouse helped one another navigate the trauma.

_____
_____
_____
_____
_____
_____
_____
_____

E. Were such a painful incident to occur again, **what would you do differently <u>during</u> the trial?**

_____
_____
_____
_____
_____
_____
_____
_____

AFTER

"This is the transition *from an inward focus*, which is necessary and understandable while working through the initial grief and loss process, *to an outward focus* keyed to contribution and comfort to others." (*Resilience God Style*, page 82, underline emphasis added)

During and in the near term following trauma, we often have many people who rally around us (perhaps military doctors and chaplains, perhaps family members when losing a loved one, perhaps your church or small community of friends, etc). As we seek to transition to a "new normal," the path often gets rockier and steeper. "Bouncing back is the most dangerous phase of the resilience journey." (*Resilience God Style*, page 152, underline emphasis added)

A. During the "After" phase of your trauma cited in "A" above, **did you find that your pain and grief seemed to get worse after the dust had settled?** Describe this. Were you angry, or frustrated, or discouraged that you couldn't just "get over it?"

_____
_____
_____
_____
_____
_____
_____
_____
_____
_____
_____
_____
_____
_____
_____
_____

B. **As you sought to "bounce back" how would you describe "looking back" at your traumatic event?** Did you and those around you understand the nature of the grief process? When did you feel like you could "accept" your loss? What role did faith play?

_____
_____
_____
_____
_____
_____
_____
_____
_____
_____

C. **Did you "get stuck" for days or even decades in a cycle of negative emotions?** (anger, bitterness, guilt, false guilt, despair, depression, suicidal ideation)

_____
_____
_____
_____
_____
_____
_____
_____
_____
_____

D. **As you sought to regain momentum and move into a new future, what helped you?**

E. **Can you say that you were able to "grow" from your traumatic event? Did you learn lessons and adapt to practices that made you stronger, wiser, better? Or, are you still wrestling with the aftermath?** (As a reminder, we never "forget" significant trauma in our lives, but we can learn to view it through a different lens.)

TENNIS BALL OR EGG?

To splat (like an egg) or not to splat: that is the question. Do we bounce like tennis balls, or do we fracture beyond repair?

F. If you were to be dropped (yet again) onto the hard concrete of life (i.e. a "body slam"), you could respond in two different ways.

   1) "It will hurt really bad. God and others will rally around me. I will eventually bounce back." … or …
   2) "I'm not sure I can take another kick in the gut. I have been hurt so deeply before. I feel like one more personal trauma is more than I can bear. I don't think I could possibly get back in the saddle."

Which outcome do you think represents your current "resilience factor?"
_____

Explain why:
_____
_____
_____
_____
_____
_____
_____
_____
_____
_____
_____

G. <u>As a final assessment step</u> before we dive deeply into the Resilience Life Cycle©, **consider the five elements of Comprehensive Personal Fitness™:** physical, mental, spiritual, emotional, and relational taken from Jesus' Great Commandment in Mark 12:29-31. **For each category below, describe your current "fitness" level, where you would like for your level to be, and how you might get there.**

   1) **Physical?**
      a) Currently at ___ (0-10), would like to be at ___
      b) Initial ideas on how to get there?

      _____
      _____
      _____
      _____
      _____
      _____
      _____
      _____

   2) **Mental?**
      a) Currently at ___ (0-10), would like to be at ___
      b) Initial ideas on how to get there?

      _____
      _____
      _____
      _____
      _____
      _____
      _____
      _____

3) **Spiritual?**

    a) Currently at ___ (0-10), would like to be at ___

    b) Initial ideas on how to get there?

_____

_____

_____

_____

_____

_____

_____

_____

4) **Emotional?**

    a) Currently at ___ (0-10), would like to be at ___

    b) Initial ideas on how to get there?

_____

_____

_____

_____

_____

_____

_____

5) **Relational?**

    a) Currently at ___ (0-10), would like to be at ___

    b) Initial ideas on how to get there?

_____

_____

_____

_____

_____

_____

_____

REGAINING ALTITUDE

This chapter of the *Resilience God Style Study Guide* represents a preliminary assessment, a current snapshot, of your resilience. Although the questions spin out of a single traumatic experience (which you described in "A" above) the full reservoir of observations about personal trauma would span across all of your traumatic life experiences to date.

After completing *Resilience God Style* and this study guide, you will have <u>a new framework by which to assess, develop, and exercise resilience in your life</u>. This pre-assessment ideally causes you to wrestle with tough questions as you dive into *Resilience God Style*, stimulating you to "be alert" to precepts and practices which will give you more bounce than before.

<u>A final note of caution</u>: This is not solely about self-effort. Certainly we do our best in each domain of Comprehensive Personal Fitness™, but the reality is that genuine trauma is beyond the sphere of mere human strength. When we dig deeply into our soul to find courage, hope, and strength in the toughest of times, we will come up empty handed without total dependence upon God the Healer through the person of Jesus Christ and the indwelling presence of God's Holy Spirit.

> "I have been crucified with Christ; and it is no longer I who live, but Christ lives in me; and the life which I now live in the flesh I live by faith in the Son of God who loved me and gave Himself up for me." (Galatians 2:20)

5
BEFORE:
Building Bounce—The Ounce of Prevention

(See *Resilience God Style*, Chapter 5)

> "This chapter has discussed how to lean in the right direction, particularly spiritually, so that we also fall in the right direction, in the direction of resilience and restoration."
> (*Resilience God Style*, page 121, summarizing why prepare for the coming storms of life).

Know Your Calling (Mission, Purpose)

"Ultimately, when the thunderbolts of life strike you and me, <u>the deep conviction of our calling in God and our calling to serve our family and fellow man, is an important anchor for the soul, a critical source of resilience</u>. At this point, I must ask: **'Do You Know Your Calling: your calling to serve God, your calling to serve man?'** These are important questions to ask and resolve now, before the chaos of trauma causes **you to question your most basic values, and God Himself."** (*Resilience God Style*, Chapter 5, page 101, underline and bold added)

A. **My Calling to Serve God:**

_____
_____
_____
_____
_____

B. **My Calling to Serve Others:**

_____
_____
_____
_____
_____

C. **My Specific Calling for this Chapter of Life**—Why am I doing what I am doing? (in the military, raising children, broadening my education? etc.)

_____
_____
_____
_____
_____

Know Your Enemy (Vulnerabilities, Threats)

"The admonition to 'know your enemy' is certainly relevant on every battlefield of life. Whether we face the enemy of self, others, inexplicable tragedy, or Satan, we must know our enemy." (*Resilience God Style*, page 106)

D. **My Personal Vulnerabilities to SIN** (lust of flesh, lust of eyes, pride of life):

_____
_____
_____
_____
_____

E. **Threats from the WORLD and Others:**

_____

_____
_____
_____
_____

F. **Threats from Supernatural Forces** (Satan, spiritual warfare, demonic beings, and unseen forces):

_____
_____
_____
_____

Know Your Friends

"Proverbs 17:17 states, 'A friend loves at all times, And a brother is born for adversity.' This passage highlights both the importance of unconditional love of friends (at all times) and the role of family (a brother) who in God's divine order is best suited to provide love, nurture, and support during difficult times. Whether the source of such friendship lies within our earthly families (prayerfully that is the case for each of us), or within a small circle of intimate friends outside the family, the implication is the same: we all need friends, particularly in times of adversity."
(*Resilience God Style*, Chapter 5, page 108)

G. **My "911" friends and family** (list **5** with any needed contact information)

1) _____
2) _____
3) _____
4) _____
5) _____

H. **My Resilience God Style "Battle Buddy"** for working through this Study Guide is:

_____

Know Your Equipment (Armor of God)

"Consider this command from a fictitious military leader: 'Okay, troops. Now ground all your equipment. We are going into combat, but I don't think you'll need all that stuff. Yes, I'm not kidding… leave your helmets, your weapons, your flak vests… leave it all behind.' We would rightly think this leader was 'off his rocker,' yet personally and collectively we frequently don't use the equipment, the soul armor that God provides to each of us." (Armor of God, Ephesians 6:14-18)
(*Resilience God Style*, Chapter 5, page 110)

I. Gird your loins with **TRUTH**—What truths can I cling to when the bottom falls out?

_____
_____
_____
_____
_____

J. Put on the Breastplate of **RIGHTEOUSNESS**—What right values and actions do I pursue to stay on the moral high ground?

_____
_____
_____
_____
_____

K. Shod your feet with the **GOSPEL OF PEACE**—Jesus is the Prince of Peace. How do I promote peace in word and deed, even as a warrior on life's battlefields?

_____
_____
_____
_____
_____

L. Taking up the **SHIELD OF FAITH**—Hebrews 11:1: "Now faith is the assurance of things hoped for, the conviction of things not seen." How do I use "eyes of faith" to have "vision" to pull me past the traumas of life?

_____

_____

_____

_____

_____

_____

M. Take the **HELMET OF SALVATION**—Jesus Christ came that we "...may have life and have it abundantly." (John 10:10b) Have I made a personal decision to ask Jesus to be the Lord and Savior of my life? If so, summarize below. If not, what would it look like for you to take this step?

_____

_____

_____

_____

_____

_____

N. Take the **SWORD OF THE SPIRIT** (Word of God)

"I was suddenly very motivated to study the Word of God, to learn it, and to make it my own by investing in scripture memory. This spiritual discipline became a critical element of preparation for warfare: in life and in the military. Little did I know how this small investment up front would impact my life and service, and provide a form of compound interest which continues to pay dividends to this day." (*Resilience God Style*, Chapter 5, page 111, Cadet Bob Dees standing over the grave of 1LT Jon Shine)

What specific sections of scripture are so relevant to you that you will commit (or already have committed) to memorizing them? (Examples for *Resilience God Style* might include: Psalm 18, 27, 34, 91, 139, Isaiah 40, Matthew 5-7, Romans 12, 2 Corinthians 4, Hebrews 12, and James 1)

1) _____

2) _____

3) _____

4) _____

5) _____

6) _____

7) _____

8) _____

9) _____

10) _____

O. **PRAY** at all times—See template below to help you be more intentional in your prayer life. The acronym "ACTS" (Adoration, Confession, Thanksgiving, Supplication) may be a useful tool for you. <u>Adoration</u>: highlight and honor God's character and attributes, often using key passages of scripture which focus on praise to God. <u>Confession</u>: agree with God that you have fallen short, consistent with 1 John 1:9 that "If we confess our sins, He is faithful and righteous to forgive us our sins and to cleanse us from all unrighteousness." <u>Thanksgiving</u>: express gratitude to God for specific areas of your life where He has been gracious to bless you or to protect you from negative outcomes. <u>Supplication</u>: ask God to meet the deepest needs of your life, consistent with Philippians 4:19: "And my God will supply all of your needs according to His riches in glory in Christ Jesus."

CONSISTENT AND COMPREHENSIVE PRAYER

	SUNDAY	MONDAY	TUESDAY	WEDNESDAY	THURSDAY	FRIDAY	SATURDAY
ADORATION	Psalm 150						
CONFESSION				--- Anything Separating You From God ---			
THANKSGIVING		Family	Job				
SUPPLICATION				Philippians 4:19			
--FAMILY		Grandchildren			Son's Family		
--FRIENDS						Battle Buddy	
--CO-WORKERS		Co-worker 1					
--CHURCH		Youth Program					Pastor
--COMMUNITY			Violence				
--LEADERS				Congress		President	
--NATIONAL			Elections		Unemployment		
--INTERNAITONAL		Missionaries		Africa			
--SELF				Writing			Matt 6:33

Examples provided in italics. Fill in each day to focus your prayers.

Deploy with the Right Mindset

"*Deploy with the Right Mindset* implies starting with the right stance to maximize your chances of staying in balance when the unexpected occurs. Certainly this makes sense in physical endeavors, but it is even more important in the mental, emotional, and spiritual dimensions. What does this look like?" (*Resilience God Style*, page 116)

P. How do you nurture your **"Attitude of Gratitude"** on a daily basis?

_____
_____
_____
_____
_____

Q. Is your personal **"Resilience Playlist"** of nurturing music compiled and available through your smart phone, or your audio player, or your computer? Insure the songs are ones which give you courage, inspire you to excel, cause you to dream, comfort you in your sorrows, and bring out the best in your heart, soul, and spirit. If you still need to do this, use space below to start brainstorming and then follow through.

1) Evans, Darrell. "Trading My Sorrow," as contained in Freedom. Nashville: Integrity/Columbia, 1998. (My #1)

2) New Song. "Sheltering Trees," as recorded in Sheltering Tree. Nashville: Benson Records, 2004. (My #2)

3) Maranatha! Music. An Invitation to Comfort: A Healing Journey Through Grief. Narrated by Dr. Tim Clinton. Nashville: Maranatha! Music, 2008. CD. (My #3)

4) Song _____

5) Song _____

6) Song _____

7) OTHERS...

Develop and Rehearse "Actions on Contact" (Get Ready!)

"So it is with us all as warriors on the journey of life. We must consider the 'Actions on Contact' that we can develop ahead of time, to increase the likelihood of resilient responses to the reality of trauma in our lives. What do we do when the body slam occurs, when we are extremely vulnerable, perhaps disillusioned, disoriented, hurt, betrayed, asking, 'Why?'" (*Resilience God Style*, page 121)

See DURING section for your "Actions on Contact."

REGAINING ALTITUDE

This chapter has addressed the "Before" phase, the period of preparation that proves to be the "ounce of prevention worth a pound of cure." In essence, we seek to stimulate spiritual transformation (known as justification) and spiritual formation (known as sanctification) <u>before</u> the next body slam occurs to you or those you lead.

> "Finally, be strong in the Lord and in the strength of His might.
> <u>Put on the full armor of God</u>, so that you will be able to stand firm against the schemes of the devil.
> (Ephesians 6: 10, 11, underline emphasis added)

6
Weathering the Storm

(See *Resilience God Style*, Chapter 6)

> "The Bible also has much to offer the wounded warrior, or the "Gold Star Mother" who has lost her son to combat, the struggling businessman, the unsuspecting cancer victim, and so many others who are suddenly beset by trauma and tribulation.
>
> The Bible doesn't sugarcoat these realities. It tells the stories of people who are just like us; their stories are just like ours." (*Resilience God Style*, page 126)

Call 911 (Ask for Help)

"Note: Your first call may actually be to the emergency number, 911, to request immediate medical care or support from police or fire personnel. For many, such an emergency call will not be warranted, yet other types of '911 calls' will be absolutely essential." (*Resilience God Style*, page 129)

A. **Pray to God.**

1) **Consider a prayer such as this:**

   "Father, I cry out to you. Help me. I don't understand this... this is really ugly... but I know you love me and will carry me through whatever this situation brings. I love you too... and I trust you... I know you give and you take away... blessed be your holy name. Give me wisdom... and courage... and integrity... and staying power to weather this storm. I can't

possibly thank you <u>for</u> this, Lord… but in obedience I thank you <u>in</u> this situation. I honor you as the sovereign King of Kings, and my Rock, Fortress, and Deliverer. Now help me to do what needs to be done. In Jesus name, Amen."

2) Or, **write your own emergency prayer** which captures what you want to tell God and what you want to ask of Him when "the bottom has fallen out" of your world:

_____
_____
_____
_____
_____
_____
_____
_____

B. **Ask for help from your most trusted family and friends.** Immediately call/text/email your "911 Friends" which you identified in "BEFORE." (Consider asking the first one you call to mobilize the others; you may not have the time, focus, or ability to call others.)

1) (Call First) _____
2) _____
3) _____
4) _____
5) _____

C. **Ask for help from professionals.**
1) Chaplain/Pastor _____ @ _____
2) Local Counselor _____ @ _____
3) Other _____ @ _____

D. **Accept help from others who have a heart to help.**

   1) Local Church(es):

      ❖ _____
      ❖ _____

   2) Local Community Organizations:

      ❖ _____
      ❖ _____

   3) Your Employer or School:

      ❖ _____
      ❖ _____

   4) If a Veteran, local Veterans Service Organizations (VSO) or Veterans Affairs (VA) Facility:

     (VSO) _____
     (VSO) _____
     Local Vet Center _____
     Local VA Hospital _____

   5) Others?

_____
_____
_____
_____
_____
_____
_____
_____

Start the IV (Nurture Yourself)

   E. **Draw courage, strength, and wisdom from repeating Scripture** which you have stored in your heart. **(Chapter 5, BEFORE, Section N of this study guide)**

   F. **Read Scripture (intensively)** for comfort, example, and inspiration. Start with the following:

   1) Psalm 23   My takeaway is:
   _____
   _____
   _____

   2) Psalm 91   My takeaway is:
   _____
   _____
   _____

   3) Psalm 18   My takeaway is:
   _____
   _____
   _____

   4) Psalm 57   My takeaway is:
   _____
   _____
   _____

   5) Psalm 34   My takeaway is:
   _____
   _____
   _____

6) 2 Corinthians, Chapters 1 – 4   My takeaways are:

_____

_____

_____

_____

_____

_____

7) Hebrews Chapters 11 and 12   My takeaways are:

_____

_____

_____

_____

_____

_____

8) Book of Philippians   My takeaways are:

_____

_____

_____

_____

_____

9) Isaiah, Chapters 40 and 41   My takeaways are:

_____

_____

_____

_____

_____

_____

10) Others?

 ❖ _____
 ❖ _____
 ❖ _____

Keep Breathing (Maintain Routines)

"So it is in a spiritual sense. To the best of your ability, <u>keep doing what you know to do</u>: keep breathing, follow your training. <u>Spiritually fit and resilient warriors will reflexively continue to exercise spiritual disciplines.</u> (*Resilience God Style*, page 135, underline emphasis added)

G. **Use your Equipment.** Keep on your "spiritual armor." Review *Resilience God Style*, Chapter 5, pages 110-116, and this *Study Guide* Chapter 5, Sections I-O, pages 65-69.

As bullet reminders from Ephesians 6: Loins girded with TRUTH, Breastplate of RIGHTEOUSNESS, feet shod with the preparation of the GOSPEL OF PEACE, shield of FAITH, helmet of SALVATION, sword of the SPIRIT (which is the WORD of GOD), all within an attitude of PRAYER and VIGILANCE.

1) While you are "weathering the storm," it will be useful to press into the Word of God to better understand the reality that "God will supply all your needs according to His riches in glory in Christ Jesus." (Philippians 4:19) In this vein, **what topic study should you do during this storm to provide focus and illumination from God?**

_____
_____
_____

2) **Although all are important, which piece of the "Armor of God" is most relevant and needed in your current situation? Why did you select this one?**

_____
_____
_____

H. **Get the praise and worship going**. Note: you probably won't feel like it at first, but praise and worship are your keys to overcoming anger, bitterness, fear, and the many negative emotions that accompany trauma.

1) **Start using your "Resilience Playlist."** Let music nurture your soul. (*Resilience God Style*, pages 119 and 120, and Section Q in Chapter 5 of this *Study Guide,* page 70)

2) **Verbalize praise to God and others**, as well as <u>giving thanks for "what did not happen:"</u>

    ❖ _____
    ❖ _____
    ❖ _____
    ❖ _____

Follow I Thessalonians 5:16-18, "Rejoice always; pray without ceasing; <u>in everything give thanks</u>, for this is God's will for you in Christ Jesus." (underline emphasis added) As with Paul and Silas in prison, practice <u>giving thanks in everything</u> in the storm:

    ❖ _____
    ❖ _____
    ❖ _____
    ❖ _____

I. **Count Your Way** through the physical, emotional, and spiritual pain. Force yourself to observe the basics of a healthy lifestyle. Maintain the following disciplines while "the storm is passing by":

1) **Physical Exercise:** Maintain your normal frequency, or consider "turning up the volume" to assist with stress reduction and better sleep (often the first casualty in a crisis).

    ❖ My Commitment is:

    _____
    _____

_____
_____
_____

2) **Spiritual Exercise:** Maintain devotional times, prayer, spiritual reflection, and journaling (next section).

   ❖ My Commitment is:

   _____
   _____
   _____
   _____
   _____

J. **Breathe spiritually** to exhale emotional, mental, and spiritual toxins and to inhale spiritual truths (including the indwelling presence of the Holy Spirit).

1) **Exhale:**

   ❖ Sin in my own life? (Confess/Ask Forgiveness)

   _____
   _____
   _____
   _____

   ❖ Emotional abuse from others? (Friends, Antagonists, Media, Others?)

   _____
   _____
   _____
   _____

   ❖ Loosen your grip (practice by symbolically opening your hands) on anger, guilt, bitterness, false guilt… as well as pride, control, power, influence, et al). I loosen my grip on the following:

_____
_____
_____
_____
_____

2) **Inhale:**

   ❖ God's Forgiveness for sinful actions and attitudes

   ❖ Indwelling Presence of the Holy Spirit

   ❖ Comfort of the Holy Spirit

   ❖ Forgiveness of Others (to be expanded in AFTER), starting with the following people from whom I have suffered offense:

   _____
   _____
   _____
   _____

K. **Hit a Knee**

   1) **Recognize that this is not "business as normal."** Adjust your near-term schedule in the following ways:

      ❖ _____
      ❖ _____
      ❖ _____
      ❖ _____

   2) **Admit the reality of your physical, emotional, spiritual, mental, or relational wounds.** Do not let real or perceived stigma keep you from "hitting a knee" in order to recover from the immediate impacts of a life trauma. Commit to getting help in the following areas:

- ❖ _____
- ❖ _____
- ❖ _____
- ❖ _____

L. **Record the Journey**

While this *Resilience God Style Battle Book* is an excellent tool for getting prepared to weather trauma and to bounce back higher than before without getting stuck, it does not replace <u>a daily journal as a way to "think out loud" with God and with yourself</u>.

"Your journal becomes a very personal and intimate way to cry out to God in writing. Many times when the shock of trauma locks up our emotions and injects doubt about foundational values, the practice of journaling or recording the journey becomes useful therapy and a practical way to reassert faith and objective truth when the ground is shaking beneath us." (*Resilience God Style*, page 138)

- ❖ **My Commitment to journal consistently before, during, and after the storms of life:**

_____
_____
_____

Draw from Your Well of Courage (Past Experiences)

"<u>Courage is the ability to overcome fear to accomplish a daunting task, honorably to the best of your ability</u>. The question then is how to courageously overcome fear in the first moments and days of trauma and crisis.

"God provided a simple equation in those days of financial catastrophe: FEAR + FAITH = COURAGE. So it is in every endeavor of life, with FAITH as the "secret sauce" for so many of us. <u>This faith has many components which fuel our wells of courage, our reservoirs of resilience</u>. Most important is ultimate faith in God, as we previously discussed Jesus calming the raging storm for his frightful disciples who needed more faith in God's sovereignty and willingness and capacity to protect them in and through the storm." (*Resilience God Style*, page 139, underline emphasis added)

M. **Review your Journal** from past weeks, months, years, and decades (if you have this rich treasury to draw upon), **to determine past life experiences** where God and others have given you courage, have brought you through trauma to a place of rest, recovery, strength, and optimism, and to a full well of courage.

Examples in my life are:

1) _____
2) _____
3) _____
4) _____
5) _____

N. **What refills my well of courage?**

1) _____
2) _____
3) _____
4) _____
5) _____

O. **Read Biblical Examples of Courage and Resilience:**

1) **Warrior David** 1 Samuel 16 - 2 Samuel 24   My takeaways:

_____
_____
_____
_____

2) **Apostle Paul** Acts 13-28   My takeaways:

_____
_____

___

3) **Others?**

___
___
___
___

Remember Your Calling

"Remembering the noble purposes that we have dedicated our lives to becomes an important anchor for our soul and vector for our future, an important ingredient that helps us maintain hope and direction amidst crisis." (*Resilience God Style,* Chapter 6, page 141)

Now, look back to Chapter 5, section A-C, pages 49-50 to <u>remember what you said before the storm hit</u>. Certainly your trauma could change some of the specifics of your future, but <u>your basic life calling does not change with trauma or tragedy</u>.

P. **My Calling to Serve God:**

___
___
___
___
___
___

Q. **My Calling to Serve Others:**

___
___
___

_____

_____

R. **My Specific Calling for this chapter of life**—Why am I doing what I am doing (in the military, raising children, broadening my education, starting a business, running a ministry, etc.)?

_____

_____

_____

_____

_____

REGAINING ALTITUDE

Chapter 5 looked at how to "build bounce" in advance for a right response to trauma, and Chapter 6 has discussed how we "weather the storm." We have provided some "best practices" along the way; you no doubt can add others to your arsenal. Now we shift gears to the difficult task of "bouncing back, without getting stuck, and even higher!" (Chapters 7 and 8)

A final word as you proceed: <u>for some of you, this "weathering the storm" section is far more than academic or preparatory</u>. Some of you are "in the pit" right now. You may be clinging to your last vestige of hope, or sanity. Some of you are down for the count, on the hard concrete, wondering if you can ever get up. As with Sharon and Deacon Collins in *Resilience God Style* (pages 142-146), you need to know that Faith, Family, and Friends will see you through. For now, it may be all you can do to cry out like the Warrior David in Psalm 57 (below), but there will be a brighter day. We next discuss how to get there.

> "Be gracious to me, O God, be gracious to me, for my soul takes refuge in You; and in the shadow of Your wings I will take refuge until the destruction passes by." (Psalm 57:1)

7
Bouncing Back...Without Getting Stuck

(See *Resilience God Style*, Chapter 7)

> "Bouncing back is the most dangerous phase of the resilience journey. 'Building Bounce' on sunny days before the storm hits is hard work, and 'Weathering the Storm' is very painful for a short and intense time when comforters are usually gathered about. 'Bouncing Back' is the most dangerous and the most challenging. This process takes the longest, it is often the loneliest path, and it is fraught with many landmines (potential sticking points) along the way."
> (*Resilience God Style*, Chapter 7, page 152)

Yet, there is hope. There are key principles you can follow to allow you to bounce back, without getting stuck, and even higher than before.

This chapter looks back, helping you to dive deeper into your primary relationships, your attitudes of forgiveness and gratitude, and your process of grieving loss (loss of a loved one, a dream, or a part of who you might have become).

Guard Your Primary Relationships

    A. **Press into God.** The three primary reasons are listed below (*Resilience God Style*, Chapter 7, beginning on page 158). Reflect on what this means in your specific situation:

1) **He is Able.**

   _____
   _____
   _____
   _____

2) **He gives us Staying Power.**

   _____
   _____
   _____
   _____

3) **He is the Healer.**

   _____
   _____
   _____
   _____

B. **Preserve Primary Relationships with Others**

"Ironically, our closest loved ones sometimes take the full blast of anger, venting, and even violence. It is imperative that we resist this tendency and temptation toward such actions which serve to alienate our closest supporters at the time we need them the most." (*Resilience God Style*, Chapter 7, page 163)

1) **Your spouse** (if married): How do you see yourself venting or distancing from your spouse? How can you "reframe" this to insure that you attribute the pain and stress to the situation, not towards your life partner? How do you reaffirm them?

   _____
   _____
   _____

2) **Your closest friends** (same questions as above):

3) **Helping your supporters maintain perspective:**

"They also have been wounded by your trauma, and they are sometimes inclined to strike out in anger or vengeance or frustration or pain on your behalf. In this case, you may find yourself as a voice of reason, one who must counsel forgiveness, gratitude, adopting a patient and reasoned approach, and ultimately love and acceptance towards the perceived source of the woundedness." (*Resilience God Style*, Chapter 7, page 164)

Has this become an issue as you have navigated your recovery from trauma? How have you dealt with it?

Choose Forgiveness and Gratitude

   C. **Flee a Spirit of Offense.**

"One of the temptations we all face when we have been body slammed is to entertain such a Spirit of Offense. Such a mindset certainly disrupts personal peace and collective unity, and it definitely heads us in the wrong direction emotionally and spiritually. Hence, this is a situation, an attitude, a mindset, a spirit we should flee from." (*Resilience God Style*, Chapter 7, page 167)

What specific actions do you need to take to flee a Spirit of Offense? Note: Appendix 4 contains a short treatise on "Fleeing a Spirit of Offense."

_____
_____
_____
_____
_____

   D. **Pursue a Spirit of Forgiveness.**

Consider Peter's interchange with Jesus again (Matt 18:21, 21): "Then Peter came and said to Him, 'Lord, how often shall my brother sin against me and I forgive him? Up to seven times?' Jesus said to him, 'I do not say to you, up to seven times, but up to seventy times seven.'"

Have you received a negative report through a third party recently that "got your blood pressure up" or caused you to assume the worst about another person? If so, how could you have handled this better?

_____
_____
_____
_____
_____
_____

Do you have a persistent "root of bitterness" from your experiences in the military, or from other life situations? If so, what steps can/should you take, ideally supported by your battle buddy in this process, to achieve true forgiveness and freedom?

1) _____
2) _____
3) _____
4) _____
5) _____

As a final reminder, "Such forgiveness is absolutely critical to 'getting unstuck' and moving on to a joyful future." (*Resilience God Style*, Chapter 7, page 171)

E. **Choose Gratitude.**

Do you have an "attitude of gratitude?" Let's practice. I'm grateful/thankful for (or "in") the following areas:

GOD

_____
_____

FAMILY

_____
_____

FRIENDS

_____
_____

PRICKLY PEOPLE

_____
_____

CIRCUMSTANCES

1) Positive:

_____
_____
_____
_____
_____

2) Adverse: (Now it is getting harder!) Remember: "in everything give thanks, for this is God's will for you in Christ Jesus." (I Thessalonians 5:18, underline added)

_____
_____
_____
_____
_____

Grieve Well

"In essence, that is a primary focus of this entire book: identifying positive, biblically-based, proactive, and reactive steps toward trauma that lead to new meaning and positive contribution as one bounces back. Said another way, we are wise to invite God into our grief process because: 'The Lord is near to the brokenhearted and saves those who are crushed in spirit.'" (Psalm 34:18) (*Resilience God Style*, Chapter 7, page 162)

F. **How are you inviting God into your grief process?**

_____
_____
_____
_____
_____

G. **Are you trying to avoid, or "stuff," the grief process?**

_____
_____
_____
_____
_____

H. **Knowing that grieving takes time, are you granting yourself "grace" as you slowly recover and restore? Or, are you impatient with yourself that waves of grief, remorse, anger are still triggered by your memories and interactions?**

_____
_____
_____
_____
_____
_____

At this point, it might be useful to re-read the section on "Grieve Well" in *Resilience God Style* (pages 173-178), as well as the Bounce Builders and Additional Study sections at the end of *Resilience God Style*, Chapter 7. In particular, note *An Invitation to Comfort: A Healing Journey Through Grief*, narrated by Dr. Tim Clinton.

REGAINING ALTITUDE

In this chapter we have seen the importance of guarding our primary relationships, choosing forgiveness and gratitude, and grieving well. These three practices counter the primary sticking points as we respond to trauma.

While we are anxious to start looking forward, we should take care to avoid (and if needed, to mend) broken relationships, the cancerous impact of anger and bitterness, and the delayed impacts of "stuffing" grief. As we depend upon God to do a healing work in us, He can (and will) help us avoid the detrimental physical, mental, spiritual, emotional, and relational impacts of "getting stuck." He can help us begin to look forward into a bright future (Chapter 8).

> "Therefore, you too have grief now; but I will see you again, and your heart will rejoice; and no one will take your joy from you."
>
> (John 16:22, Christ commenting on transformation from grief to joy)

8
Bouncing Ahead...Into a Hopeful Future

(See *Resilience God Style*, Chapter 8)

> "As we continue our discussion of "Bouncing Back," it is of uppermost importance for us to not miss the mark as we contemplate and envision the hopeful future that God has planned for each us. No doubt we could all have a pretty good "pity party," but let's spend some time on the other side of the ledger." (*Resilience God Style,* page 183)

This chapter looks forward, helping you to navigate new beginnings. It is inherently more process focused, providing techniques for exploring future lifestyle, vocations, and avocations. It may simply result in a validation of the azimuth you were on before trauma or tragedy reared its ugly head, or it may result in a significant life change that will require vision, boldness, courage, and perseverance to navigate. In either instance, the desired result is a sense of anticipation, a sense that the best is yet to come, a sense that God will truly turn your mourning into a joyful, hopeful and productive future.

We now look at singing a new song, revalidating your calling, and comforting others.

Sing a New Song

"Hence, a critical element in 'Bouncing Back' without getting stuck is <u>the recovery of 'vital optimism' and the recovery of hope for a brighter future</u>. Part of this process is <u>learning to sing a new song</u>, a metaphor I will use for the broader concept of being renewed in body, mind, soul, spirit, and relationships as we rise from the ashes of brokenness." (*Resilience God Style*, Chapter 8, page 185, underline added)

A. **What picture does the word "new" form in your mind? Reflect on "the power of new."**

_____
_____
_____
_____
_____
_____
_____
_____
_____
_____

B. **Now consider what the Bible says about "new."** Try a short topic study, looking at Isaiah 43:19, 2 Corinthians 5:17, Mark 2:22, Hebrews 10:20, Isaiah 62:2, Lamentations 3:22, 23; Romans 12:2, and others. Record your observations here:

_____
_____
_____
_____
_____
_____
_____
_____
_____
_____

C. **Keep looking for the return of your "vital optimism."** Are there any ideas, activities, or appropriate new relationships which have begun to spark your imagination and cause you to look forward with new anticipation?

_____
_____
_____
_____
_____
_____
_____

"If we are to 'bounce back and not get stuck,' then we must at some point 'sing a new song' which may include actual singing, but more importantly new beginnings, new dreams, new life-giving relationships, and new depth of meaning and purpose with the God who created you, loves you, and has good plans for you in the future." (*Resilience God Style*, Chapter 8, page 188, underline added)

Revalidate Your Calling (Discern and Chart the Future)

D. **Establish a Personal Board of Directors.**

"In essence, for times of decision and transition one creates a small group, consisting of three or four couples, that constitutes your personal board for a predetermined, limited duration. As mentioned previously, when one is rebounding, they are particularly vulnerable to making premature or unwise life decisions. Hence, making yourself and your spouse open and accountable to this small 'board' of friends is extremely valuable." (*Resilience God Style*, Chapter 8, page 189)

Who should be on your personal "board of directors?" How will you meet? How long will this advisory group provide input, apart from ongoing friendship and close fellowship?

- ❖ _____
- ❖ _____
- ❖ _____
- ❖ _____

To provide structure for your personal decision making, consider the following processes (described in detail in Chapter 8) as projects to do with your spouse or closest friend, prior to receiving input from your personal board.

E. **Lay out your "personal fixed costs." (Balanced Living)** Starting with a clean slate, look at the "fixed costs" of one's life, the "must do's," the true priorities. We call this your **"Values Map."** "This is an ideal way to view something we will call Comprehensive Personal Fitness (CPF), the balanced and prioritized integration of the emotional (heart), spiritual (soul), mental (mind), physical (strength), and relational (your 'neighbor,' starting with family and friends) aspects of your life." (*Resilience God Style*, Chapter 8, page 191)

The spaces below will get you started, but I have found it useful to lay these out on large sheets of paper ("butcher paper") to allow plenty of room for you and your board to see, discuss, brainstorm, and help you converge on <u>something that makes sense for you</u>.

PHYSICAL

_____

_____

MENTAL

_____

_____

SPIRITUAL

_____

_____

EMOTIONAL

_____

_____

RELATIONAL

_____

_____

Don't forget to assess how much time and energy this takes. This determines what remaining hours you have in your typical day/week/year to devote to your "personal variable costs."

"This exercise is also an important reminder that there is a very real cost to such a grounded and balanced lifestyle, but that the rewards are incalculable particularly for one who is bouncing back or in a major life transition." (*Resilience God Style*, Chapter 8, page 192)

F. **Lay out your "personal variable costs."** We call this a **"Mission Map."**

"With the remaining time left in one's year, including the time devoted to rest, one then budgets the variable costs. These are decisions over which we have full control, consisting of the discretionary allocation of remaining time, passion, and energies across personal and professional domains." (*Resilience God Style*, Chapter 8, page 192)

Again, some spaces are provided below to get you started, but this exercise lends itself to large sheets of paper or a whiteboard which facilitate brainstorming, visual patterns, and "aha" moments.

1) **Identify your known personal assets**: competencies, passions, areas of deep experience and accomplishment, and academic strengths. List for vocationally (professional work experience) and non-vocationally (hobbies, non-profit participation, recreation).

_____

_____

_____

_____

_____

_____

_____

2) **Identify vocational <u>options</u> and <u>options you would like to have</u>** that represent a good intersection of your distinctives above.

_____

_____

_____

_____

_____

_____

3) **Do the same for non-vocational options.**

_____

_____

_____

_____

_____

_____

4) **Craft Scenarios** which represent <u>realistic time commitments</u>, and the best intersections of your personal assets with your vocational/non-vocational options. Without a doubt, this is the "creative" part of the exercise; your personal board of directors will be very helpful here.

Scenarios might look like the following:

Vocation:

    Work for Company A (75% = _____ man days/year)

    Consult for Company B (10% = _____ man days/year)

Non-vocation:

    Help Non-Profit X (10% = _____ man day/year)

    Serve on Non-Profit Y Board (5% = _____ man day/year)

"The overall objective of this personal and professional budgeting drill is obviously to deal with the reality of limited time and limited capacity. Obtaining wisdom from the personal board of directors is particularly valuable during this stage. Assuming you are sufficiently open and vulnerable, they will provide the invaluable 'wisdom of many counselors' (Proverbs 15:22) as they help you be sufficiently introspective regarding the why and how of the future life options you are considering." (*Resilience God Style*, Chapter 8, page 194, underlines added)

Comfort Others

"Not only does God love us and comfort us, He also has higher purposes for our suffering so that we may comfort others. As we do this, God accelerates our own healing process, largely because our focus turns from our own travails to the rewarding opportunity to help others." (*Resilience God Style*, Chapter 8, page 196, underlines added)

    G. **When have you seen this biblical principle in practice? Do you have an example from your past?**

_____
_____
_____
_____
_____

H. **Who might <u>you be able to help now</u>, even while in your own painful recovery?**

❖ _____

❖ _____

❖ _____

I. **When possible, start to carry your load again.** "We need help, and there are many around us who are glad to share the burden. We should, however, <u>attempt to 'pull our own weight,'</u> carry our own rucksack <u>as soon as possible</u>; and to begin to lend a shoulder to the collective team effort for the benefit of others. <u>Otherwise, we 'get stuck' in persistent dependency</u> on others with the peripheral downside of co-dependency on the part of our closest caregivers. Comforting others <u>moves us away from any vestige of an unhealthy, lingering victim mentality</u>, and ushers us into new realms as healthy caregivers." (*Resilience God Style*, Chapter 8, page 199, underlines added)

Here are some ways I can begin to shoulder some of the load for those around me:

_____
_____
_____
_____

J. **Stewardship of Pain**

"The principle is this: In life, <u>we find different things in our hands</u>: wealth, influence, access, gifts, and talents. We are called <u>to take what is in our hands, release our grip, and allow God to use our meager offerings to His glory</u>, for the benefit of others.

This applies equally to the '<u>stewardship of pain</u>.' As we pry our fingers loose from our violated rights, our broken dreams, our inexplicable tragedies, <u>God takes our life experiences and multiplies them for good in the lives of others</u>. And, we get the joy of being an instrument of healing in the life of another; one of life's 'priceless' gifts." (*Resilience God Style*, Chapter 8, page 198, underlines added)

What do you hold in your hands? Are you able to release your grip on pain, injustice, and trauma in your life so that God can multiply it for the benefit of others? **Express your thoughts about this.**

_____
_____
_____
_____
_____
_____
_____

REGAINING ALTITUDE

By this time, you should better appreciate the need for a "battle buddy" or a small group to process all of this with. Basically, this is "hard work," but you are making an investment that will pay off for the rest of your earthly life, and beyond.

By now, you should also have a better appreciation that such life transformation is not just hard, it is absolutely impossible without the transforming power of God. He truly can turn our mourning to joy, our joy to strength, and our strength to service. And He can and will do this more than once… for we will surely need it.

Now we look at the Resilience Life Cycle© feedback loop. How do we learn and adapt, how do we "Get Ready" <u>again</u>? Chapter 9 of this *Resilience God Style Study Guide* helps us dissect that process.

Hang in there! We have almost completed our "first lap around the track." We can do it… together… with God.

> "Therefore, I urge you, brethren, by the mercies of God, to <u>present your bodies a living and holy sacrifice</u>, acceptable to God, which is your spiritual service of worship. And do not be conformed to this world, but be <u>transformed by the renewal of your mind</u>, so that you may prove what the will of God is, <u>that which is good and acceptable and perfect</u>."
> (Romans 12:1, 2; underline emphasis added)

9
Learn and Adapt: Getting Ready...Again!

(See *Resilience God Style*, Chapter 9)

> From *Resilience God Style*, Chapter 9, page 211:
> "Take the areas we highlighted as instrumental in Building Bounce (Chapter 5, *Resilience God Style*) and determine how you might learn and adapt within each of these readiness factors as you integrate the lessons learned."

In each of the sections below, record your own "Learn and Adapt" observations:

A. ***Know Your Calling.*** Has your recent trauma given you new insight on your gifts, your passions, and your sense of God's direction regarding how he can uniquely grow you and use you?

_____
_____
_____
_____
_____
_____
_____
_____

B. ***Know Your Enemy.*** You have learned new things about yourself. **What are the weaknesses and vulnerabilities you should be more aware of in the future? How do you reduce risk in these areas**, particularly the three categories listed in 1 John 2:16 (underlining added)**:** "For all that is in the world, the lust of the flesh and the lust of the eyes, and the boastful pride of life, is not from the Father, but is from the world." You have also learned more about others on your traumatic journey. Who can you trust? Who and what must you be cautious about? As well, you have become wiser about spiritual warfare and the Evil One "which wages war against your soul."

_____
_____
_____
_____
_____
_____
_____

C. ***Know Your Friends.*** Some of your "friends" probably headed the other direction when adversity camped on your doorstep, and some friends were "closer than a brother." (Proverbs 18:4) This is useful information for facing the future battles of life. **Who do you now trust to cover your back? Who will be a reliable battle buddy in coming days? Who do you want to "grow old with" in friendship and service together? What relationships are "life giving," and what relationships should you not continue or pursue in your next chapters of life?**

_____
_____
_____
_____
_____
_____
_____

D. **Know Your Equipment.** As you endured trauma and sought to bounce back without getting stuck, what spiritual disciplines were beneficial, which ones broke down under the stress and strain? **How do you enhance your spiritual fitness** Did you learn more about the "Armor of God?" How to wear it, use it? What specific parts of the Bible, and other edifying media were especially relevant and restorative to you? How do you make these a part of your own Bounce Builders, and **how do you consolidate these in your own life as you begin to comfort and train others?**

_____
_____
_____
_____
_____
_____
_____
_____

E. **Deploy with the Right Mindset.** Often the awareness of God's provision and comfort, as well as the love and assistance from dear family and friends, increases our gratitude quotient. **How do we capture and practice this new-found gratitude to God and others in ways that will make this a subconscious reflex? How do we choose forgiveness, recognizing that it is not a one-time event?**

_____
_____
_____
_____
_____
_____
_____
_____

F. ***Develop and Rehearse "Actions on Contact."*** Reflect again on the "Actions on Contact" recommended in Chapter 6, "Weathering the Storm." Look at each one with new insight. **Update your** *Resilience God Style Study Guide* **with the specifics which will pay dividends in the future** regarding:

> **Call 911** (crying out to God, Family and Friends, and other caregivers)
>
> **Start the IV** (intensive intake of biblical truth and inspiration)
>
> **Keep Breathing** (continue basic spiritual disciplines despite chaos)
>
> **Draw from Your Well of Courage** (reflect back on prior situations when God provided and comforted)
>
> **Remember Your Calling** (having clarified your purpose in previous iterations of life trauma so you can remind yourself of your calling when you are knocked to your knees again).

If I Could Do It Over

G. Look back at Chapter 1, Section A, pages 15-17. You identified three past traumatic life experiences. **Knowing what you know now, how would you deal differently with the Before, During, and After phases of these seismic events in your life?**

1) _____
_____
_____
_____
_____
_____
_____
_____

2) _____
_____
_____
_____
_____

3) _____

Being a Lifetime Learner

H. **How would you characterize your skills as a "lifetime learner?"** Are these strengths or weaknesses for you? Do you have an "after action review" process in place where you intentionally review personal performance, as well as seeking input from others?

GROWTH THROUGH ADVERSITY TOOL

Appendix 3 includes a Growth Through Adversity Tool that is a shorthand version of the introspective questions contained in this study guide chapter. This tool can be used by individuals or others in group settings, to process the body slams (trauma) in their lives.

REGAINING ALTITUDE

We have said many times that "with height comes perspective." This is not just true of physical or geographic altitude, but also with spiritual altitude. Having navigated this far in the Resilience Life Cycle©, you no doubt have climbed to greater spiritual heights that now afford you new perspective, and new resilience. As well, you likely have increased your emotional and relational "IQ" as well.

I maintain that "good outfits talk to themselves." We talk more about this in *Resilient Leaders* and *Resilient Nations* (www.ResilienceGodStyle.com), but this also applies to us as individuals. Ideally during this process, our "self-talk," meaning our practice of personal introspection before the Lord, has become healthier and central to our ability to bounce back.

In the words of *Resilience God Style* (page 210, underline emphasis added) "And so it is with each of us. In each of our respective foxholes of life, we fight, we get wounded, we bounce back, and we fight again, placing one boot in front of the other. As the British philosopher George Santana maintained, 'Those who fail to learn the lessons of history are destined to repeat them.' So it is in warfare. So it is in life."

> "But we have this treasure in earthen vessels, so that the surpassing greatness of the power will be of God and not from ourselves. We are afflicted in every way, but not crushed; perplexed, but not despairing; persecuted, but not forsaken; struck down, but not destroyed; always carrying about in the body the dying of Jesus, so that the life of Jesus may also be manifested in our body. For we who live are constantly being delivered over to death for Jesus' sake, so that the life of Jesus also may be manifested in our mortal flesh."
> (2 Corinthians 4:8-11)

10
Learn and Adapt: And Even Higher!

(See *Resilience God Style*, Chapter 10)

> "The bottom line is that faith matters. The Christian faith in particular makes a significant difference in success or failure, victory or defeat, and hope or despair in the lives of all warriors in every foxhole of life." (*Resilience God Style* page 229)

THE ULTIMATE RESILIENT WARRIOR—JESUS CHRIST

I challenge you to not miss the "secret sauce" in this recipe for resilience: the person of Jesus Christ.

A. **JESUS WAS THE ULTIMATE "RESILIENT WARRIOR."** Draw strength and encouragement from His example. What characteristics in the life of Jesus can you most relate with? (See Chapter 10 of *Resilience God Style* for suggestions.)

_____
_____
_____
_____
_____
_____
_____

B. **JESUS IS THE SUPREME OBJECT OF FAITH.** "The pragmatic truth is that <u>a personal relationship with God through Jesus</u>, a partnership with the <u>indwelling and comforting presence of God's Holy Spirit</u>, and <u>a strong expectation that God does and will provide comfort, wisdom, and strength</u> through the pages of the Bible are incredibly relevant and provide practical means to prepare for trauma, weather its storm, and bounce back without getting stuck, to arrive at an even higher plane of performance and life fulfillment than ever before." (*Resilience God Style*, Chapter 10, page 228, underlines added)

In who or what do you place your faith? Is this a consistent practice, or a crisis response to threatening situations?

_____
_____
_____
_____
_____
_____
_____

C. **JESUS IS THE SOURCE OF ULTIMATE HOPE.** A prayer for you and me from the Apostle Paul: "Now may the <u>God of Hope fill you with all joy and peace in believing</u>, so that you will <u>abound in hope</u> by the power of the Holy Spirit." (Romans 15:13, underlines added)

What are the sources of HOPE in your life?

_____
_____
_____
_____
_____
_____
_____

REGAINING ALTITUDE

MY *HOPE* AND *PRAYER* FOR YOU AND ME:

- That you and I will enjoy "Fair weather and following seas" (a traditional U.S Navy benediction),

- But, when the *storms of life* head our way, and they *will,*

- That you and I will be *ready*, having invested in *personal resilience,*

- So when the strong winds blow, you and I will *bend but not break,*

- That we will get *better* and not bitter,

- Become *significant survivors* and not sad statistics,

- Able to *comfort others* with that with which we have been comforted,

- Experiencing *healing, purpose, contribution,* and *joy* beyond what we ever thought possible,

- **And in the power of our Creator God that we may:**

    Bounce Back

    Without Getting Stuck

    And Even Higher!

After you have suffered for a little while, the God of all grace, who called you to His eternal glory in Christ, will Himself perfect, confirm, strengthen, and establish you."

I Peter 5:10

About the Author
ROBERT F. DEES
Major General, U.S. Army, Retired

Major General (Retired) Robert F. Dees was born in Amarillo, Texas on 2 February 1950. Graduating from the US Military Academy in 1972, he was commissioned as a second lieutenant of Infantry and awarded a Bachelor of Science degree. He also holds a Masters degree in Operations Research from the Naval Postgraduate School. His military education includes the Infantry Officer Basic and Advanced Courses, the US Army Command and General Staff College, and the Industrial College of the Armed Forces. He was also a Research Fellow at the Royal College of Defence Studies in London and was licensed as a registered Professional Engineer in the State of Virginia.

General Dees served in a wide variety of command and staff positions culminating in his last three assignments as Assistant Division Commander for Operations, 101st Airborne Division (Air Assault); Commander, Second Infantry Division, United States Forces Korea; and as Deputy Commanding General, V (US/GE) Corps in Europe, concurrently serving as Commander, US-Israeli Combined Task Force for Missile Defense. He commanded airborne, air assault, and mechanized infantry forces from platoon through division level; including two tours as company commander and regimental commander in the historic "Rakkasans," the 187th Regimental Combat Team. General Dees is a Distinguished Member of the Regiment, and has served a five-year tenure as Honorary Colonel of the Regiment for the Rakkasans.

About the Author

General Dees' awards and decorations include the Defense Distinguished Service Medal, Distinguished Service Medal (2), Legion of Merit (2), Meritorious Service Medal (6), Joint Service Commendation Medal, Army Commendation Medal, and the Republic of Korea Chonsu Order of National Security. General Dees has also been awarded the Ranger Tab, Senior Parachutist and Air Assault Badges, the Expert Infantryman's Badge, the Army Staff Identification Badge, and the Joint Staff Identification Badge. General Dees was also awarded the 2003 Centurion Award by the National Association for Evangelicals for long term support to chaplains while in command positions.

Officially retiring from the Army on 1 January 2003, he worked as Director of Homeland Security for Electronic Warfare Associates; then as Executive Director, Defense Strategies, Microsoft Corporation for two years. In that role, General Dees formulated the strategy for Microsoft's US Defense sector and engaged with leadership of Microsoft's major defense partners. In addition, he served as Microsoft lead for Reconstruction of Iraq, coordinating efforts with US Government, foreign governments, and private sector partners in the US and abroad. General Dees then served for five years (2005-2010) as Executive Director, Military Ministry providing spiritual nurture to troops and families around the world. Following this General Dees served as Associate Vice President for Military Outreach for Liberty University (leading the Liberty University Institute for Military Resilience), Military Director for the American Association of Christian Counselors, and Senior Military Advisor for DNA Military. His Resilience Trilogy books (*Resilient Warriors*, *Resilient Leaders*, and *Resilient Nations*) are used in Psychology, Counseling, Business, Religion, and Government courses at Liberty University. He has also authored *Resilience God Style*, an associated *Resilience God Style Study Guide*, a *Resilience God Style Video Series*, and a *Resilience God Style Training Game*.

General Dees also served as National Security Advisor, followed by Presidential Campaign Chairman, for Dr. Ben Carson. He is now President of Resilience Consulting, LLC, serving a variety of constituents in the arenas of resilience consulting, business, cyber defense, counterterrorism, and care for military troops and families. As well, General Dees serves on the Board of Directors of the Lindell Foundation, bringing help, hope, and healing to addicts, downtrodden veterans, and other needy populations in America and beyond.

About the Author

General Dees frequently provides leadership and resilience talks at a variety of seminars and conferences, as well as commentary on current military and resilience issues in such as FOX Huckabee, FOX Business, Council for National Policy, Focus on the Family, Christian Broadcasting Network, American Association of Christian Counselors, American Family Radio, Wildfire Men's Conferences, New Canaan Society, Pinnacle Forum, Wallbuilders Live, and numerous churches across America. He was featured as one of 30 "Master Leaders" by George Barna, and was presented the 2018 George Washington Military Leadership Award by the Council for National Policy.

General Dees is married to the former Kathleen Robinson of Houston, Texas. They have two married children and seven grandchildren, and are grateful for the privilege of continuing to serve God, Nation, and others during these critical times.

Bibliography

Adsit, Chris. *The Combat Trauma Healing Manual: Christ-centered Solutions for Combat Trauma.* Newport News, VA: Military Ministry, 2007.

Adsit, Chris, Rahnella Adsit and Marshéle Carter Waddell. *When War Comes Home: Christ-Centered Healing for Wives of Combat Veterans.* Newport News, VA: Military Ministry, 2008.

Alexander, Eric. *The Summit: Faith Beyond Everest's Death Zone.* Green Forest, AR: New Leaf, 2010.

Alley, Lee. *Back From War: Finding Hope & Understanding in Life After Combat.* With assistance from Wade Stevenson. Midlothian, VA: Exceptional, 2007.

Ambrose, Stephen. *Undaunted Courage: Meriwether Lewis, Thomas Jefferson and the Opening of the American West.* New York: Simon & Schuster, 2003.

American Bible Society. *God Understands When You Fear Death.* God Understands Series. 8 vols. (unnumbered). New York: American Bible Society, 2009.

American Bible Society. *God Understands When You Feel Angry.* God Understands Series. 8 vols. (unnumbered). New York: American Bible Society, 2009.

American Bible Society. *God Understands When You Feel Hopelessness and Despair.* God Understands Series. 8 vols. (unnumbered). New York: American Bible Society, 2009.

American Bible Society. *God Understands When You Feel Life Is Meaningless and Without Purpose.* God Understands Series. 8 vols. (unnumbered). New York: American Bible Society, 2009.

American Bible Society. *God Understands When You Feel Life Is Unfair.* God Understands Series. 8 vols. (unnumbered). New York: American Bible Society, 2009.

Bibliography

American Bible Society. *God Understands When You Feel Overwhelmed With Guilt.* God Understands Series. 8 vols. (unnumbered). New York: American Bible Society, 2009.

American Bible Society. *God Understands When You Feel Sadness and Grief.* God Understands Series. 8 vols. (unnumbered). New York: American Bible Society, 2009.

American Bible Society. *God Understands When You Have Doubts.* God Understands Series. 8 vols. (unnumbered). New York: American Bible Society, 2009.

Amos Jr., James H. *The Memorial: A Novel of the Vietnam War.* Lincoln, NE: iUniverse.com, 2001.

Antal, John. *Hell's Highway: The True Story of the 101st Airborne Division During Operation Market Garden, September 17-25, 1944.* Minneapolis: Zenith, 2008.

Archer, Bernice and Kent Fedorowich. "The Women of Stanley: internment in Hong Kong, 1942-45." *Women's History Review* 5, no. 3 (1996): 373-399.

Barclay, William, trans. *The Letters to the Corinthians.* Revised ed. Philadelphia: Westminster, 1975. First published 1954 by The Saint Andrew Press in Edinburgh, Scotland.

———, trans. *The Letters to the Galatians and Ephesians.* Philadelphia: Westminster, 1976. First published 1954 by The Saint Andrew Press in Edinburgh, Scotland.

Barton, Ruth Haley. *Strengthening the Soul of Your Leadership: Seeking God in the Crucible of Ministry.* Downers Grove, IL: InterVarsity Press / IVP Books, 2008.

Benderly, Beryl Lieff. "Deciphering Today's Signature War Injury: Without More Knowledge, TBI and PTSD Are Ticking Time Bombs." *Science Progress.* Last modified December 2, 2008. http://scienceprogress.org/2008/12/deciphering-todays-signature-war-injury/.

Bevere, John. *The Bait of Satan.* 10th Anniversary Ed. Lake Mary, FL: Charisma House, 2004.

Bonhoeffer, Dietrich. *The Cost of Discipleship.* New York: Touchstone, 1995.

———. *Letters & Papers From Prison, The Enlarged Edition.* Edited by Eberhard Bethge. New York: Touchstone, 1997.

Bradley, James. *Flags of Our Fathers.* New York: Bantam Dell, 2000.

Bibliography

Brinsfield, John W., William C. Davis, Benedict Maryniak and James I. Robertson, Jr., eds. *Faith in the Fight: Civil War Chaplains.* Mechanicsburg, PA: Stackpole Books, 2003.

Buck, Janie and Mary Lou Davis. *Flight Path: A Biography of Frank Barker Jr.* Scotland, UK: Christian Focus, 2003.

Cantrell, Bridget C. and Chuck Dean. *Down Range to Iraq and Back.* Seattle: WordSmith, 2005.

Cash, Carey H. *A Table in the Presence*. Nashville: W Publishing Group, 2004.

Charles, J. Daryl and Timothy J. Demy. *War, Peace and Christianity: Questions and Answers from a Just-War Perspective.* Wheaton, IL: Crossway, 2010.

Clark, Allen. *Wounded Soldier, Healing Warrior: A Personal Story of a Vietnam Veteran Who Lost His Legs but Found His Soul.* St. Paul, MN: Zenith, 2007.

Clinton, Tim, Archibald Hart and George Ohlschlager, eds. *Caring for People God's Way: Personal and Emotional Issues, Addictions, Grief and Trauma.* Nashville: Thomas Nelson / Nelson Reference & Electronic, 2005.

Clinton, Tim and Ron Hawkins, eds. *The Popular Encyclopedia of Christian Counseling*. Eugene, OR: Harvest House, 2011.

Cook, Jane Hampton, Jocelyn Green and John Croushorn. *Battlefields & Blessings: Stories of Faith and Courage from the War in Iraq & Afghanistan.* Chattanooga, TN: God & Country, 2009.

Coy, Colonel Jimmie Dean. *A Gathering of Eagles*. 2nd ed. Mobile, AL: Evergreen, 2004.

———. *Prisoners of Hope: A Gathering of Eagles, Book Three*. Mobile, AL: Evergreen, 2005.

———. *Valor: A Gathering of Eagles.* Mobile, AL: Evergreen, 2003.

Dees, Robert F. *Resilient Warriors.* San Diego, CA: Creative Team Publishing, 2011.

———. *Resilient Warriors Advanced Study Guide*. San Diego, CA: Creative Team Publishing, 2012.

———. *Resilient Leaders*. San Diego, CA: Creative Team Publishing, 2013.

Bibliography

———. *Resilient Nations*. San Diego, CA: Creative Team Publishing, 2014.

———. *Resilience God Style*. Ft. Worth, TX. Creative Team Publishing, 2018.

DeMoss, Nancy Leigh. *Choosing Forgiveness: Your Journey to Freedom.* Chicago: Moody, 2006.

———. *Choosing Gratitude: Your Journey to Joy.* Chicago: Moody, 2009.

Downer, Phil. *From Hell To Eternity: Life After Trauma.* Signal Mountain, TN: Eternal Impact, 2010.

"Empire Discontinued." *The Economist Newspaper Limited.* June 5, 2003. Accessed November 7, 2011. http://www.economist.com/node/1825845?story_id=1825845

Gražulis, Nijolė, trans. & ed. *The Chronicle of the Catholic Church in Lithuania,* Vol. 1. Chicago: Loyola University Press and Society for the Publication of the Chronicle of the Catholic Church in Lithuania, 1981.

———. *The Chronicle of the Catholic Church in Lithuania,* Vol. 6. Chicago: Society of the Chronicle of Lithuania, 1989.

Hedrick, David T. and Gordon Barry Davis, Jr. *I'm Surrounded by Methodists: Diary of John H. W. Stuckenberg. . . .* Gettysburg, PA: Thomas, 1995.

Hill, Margaret, Harriet Hill, Richard Bagge and Pat Miersma. *Healing the Wounds of Trauma: How the Church Can Help.* Nairobi, Kenya: Paulines Publications Africa, 2004.

Hillenbrand, Laura. *Unbroken.* New York: Random House, 2010.

Hurt, Bruce. "Romans 5:3 Commentary." P-R-E-C-E-P-T A-U-S-T-I-N. Last modified January 1, 2011. http://www.preceptaustin.org/romans_53-5.htm.

Hutchens, James M. *Beyond Combat.* Great Falls, VA: The Shepherd's Press, 1986.

Jackson Jr., Harry R. *The Warrior's Heart: Rules of Engagement for the Spiritual War Zone.* Grand Rapids: Chosen Books, 2004.

Jones, J. William. *Christ in the Camp: The True Story of the Great Revival During the War Between the States.* Harrisonburg, VA: Sprinkle, 1986.

Bibliography

Jordan, Merle R. "A Spiritual Perspective On Trauma and Treatment." *National Center for PTSD Clinical Quarterly* 5, no. 1, (Winter 1995): 9-10.

Kay, Ellie. *Heroes at Home: Help & Hope for America's Military Families.* Bloomington, MN: Bethany House, 2002.

Koenig, Harold G. *The Healing Power of Faith: How Belief and Prayer Can Help You Triumph Over Disease.* New York: Touchstone, 2001.

Kushner, Harold. *When Bad Things Happen to Good People.* New York: Anchor Books, 2004.

Lewis, C. S. *The Problem of Pain*. New York: Harper Collins, 2001. First published 1944 by Macmillan.

Light University. *Stress & Trauma Care: With Military Application.* Forest, VA: Light University, 2009. Counseling Certificate Training Program. DVD series. http://www.lightuniversity.com

Light University. *Stress & Trauma Care: With Military Application.* Forest, VA: Light University, 2009. Counseling Certificate Training Program. Workbook. http://www.lightuniversity.com

Lowney, Chris. *Heroic Leadership.* Chicago: Loyola, 2003.

Lucado, Max. *3:16: The Numbers of Hope.* Nashville: Thomas Nelson, 2007.

Lueders, Beth J. *Lifting Our Eyes: Finding God's Grace Through the Virginia Tech Tragedy; The Lauren McCain Story.* New York: Berkeley Books, 2007.

Luttrell, Marcus. *Lone Survivor: The Eyewitness Account of Operation Redwing and the Lost Heroes of Seal Team 10.* With the assistance of Patrick Robinson. New York: Little, Brown, 2007.

MacArthur, John. *The MacArthur New Testament Commentary: Romans 1-8.* Chicago: Moody, 1991.

MacDonald, Gordon. *Mid-Course Correction: Re-Ordering Your Private World for the Next Part of Your Journey.* Nashville: Thomas Nelson, 2005.

Manion, Jeff. *The Land Between: Finding God in Difficult Times.* Grand Rapids: Zondervan, 2010.

Mansfield, Stephen. *The Faith of the American Soldier.* New York: Jeremy P. Tarcher / Penguin, 2005.

Maranatha! Music. *An Invitation to Comfort: A Healing Journey Through Grief.* Narrated by Dr. Tim Clinton. Nashville: Maranatha! Music, 2008. CD.

"Medal of Honor Recipients: Vietnam (A—L)." *U.S. Army Center of Military History.* Last modified November 18, 2011. http://www.history.army.mil/html/moh/vietnam-a-l.html.

Military Ministry. *Spiritual Fitness Handbook: A Christian Perspective for Soldiers & Families.* U.S. Army ed. Newport News, VA: Military Ministry, 2010.

Miller, Chuck. *The Spiritual Formation of Leaders: Integrating Spiritual Formation and Leadership Development.* N.p.: Xulon, 2007.

Morgan, Robert J. *Then Sings My Soul: 150 of the World's Greatest Hymn Stories.* Nashville: Thomas Nelson, 2003.

Mumford, Nigel W. D. and Caroline Temple. *Hand to Hand: From Combat to Healing.* Revised ed. New York: Church, 2006.

Phillips, Michael M. *The Gift of Valor: A War Story.* New York: Broadway Books, 2005.

Pizzo, Angelo. *Rudy.* Directed by David Anspaugh. Produced by Robert N. Fried and Cary Woods. Videocassette (VHS), 112 min. Burbank, CA: Columbia Tristar Home Video, 1993.

Plekenpol, Chris. *Faith in the Fog of War.* Sisters, OR: Multnomah, 2006.

"Posttraumatic Growth: A Brief Overview." UNC Charlotte. Accessed October 27, 2011. http://ptgi.uncc.edu/whatisptg.htm.

Rayburn, Robert G. *Fight the Good Fight: Lessons From the Korean War.* Lookout Mountain, TN: Covenant College Press, 1956.

Ruth, Peggy Joyce. *Psalm 91: God's Shield of Protection.* Military ed. Kirkwood, MO: Impact Christian Books, 2005.

Schaeffer, Edith. *Affliction: A Compassionate Look at the Reality of Pain and Suffering.* Grand Rapids: Baker Books, 1993.

Bibliography

Schaeffer, Francis A. *Joshua and the Flow of Biblical History*. Downers Grove, IL: InterVarsity Press, 1977.

Schiffer, Michael. *Lean On Me*. Directed by John G. Avildsen. Produced by Norman Twain. Videocassette (VHS), 109 min. Burbank, CA: Warner Bros., 1989.

Schumacher, John W. *A Soldier of God Remembers: Memoir Highlights of A Career Army Chaplain*. Nappanee, IN: Evangel, 2000.

Secretariat. Directed by Randall Wallace. 2010. Burbank, CA: Walt Disney Studios Home Entertainment. DVD.

Segal, David R. and Mady Wechsler Segal. "America's Military Population." *Population Bulletin* 59, no. 4 (Washington, DC: Population Reference Bureau, 2004).

Self, Nate. *Two Wars: One Hero's Fight on Two Fronts—Abroad and Within*. Carol Stream, IL: Tyndale House, 2008.

Shealy, Keith. *Letters from the Front*. Yorktown, VA: Eagle Project, 2007.

Shephard, Ben. *A War of Nerves: Soldiers and Psychiatrists in the Twentieth Century*. Cambridge: Harvard University Press, 2001.

Shive, Dave. *Night Shift: God Works in the Dark Hours of Life*. Lincoln, NE: Back to the Bible, 2001.

Signorelli, Archibald. *Plan of Creation or Sword of Truth*. Chicago: Charles H Kerr & Company, 1916.

Smiley, Scotty. *Hope Unseen: The Story of the U.S. Army's First Blind Active-Duty Officer*. With Doug Crandall. New York: Howard Books, 2010.

Sorge, Bob. *Pain Perplexity and Promotion: A Prophetic Interpretation of the Book of Job*. Grandview, MO: Oasis House, 1999.

Stanley, Charles. *How to Handle Adversity*. Nashville: Thomas Nelson, 1989.

Stowell, Joseph, M. *The Upside of Down: Finding Hope When It Hurts*. Grand Rapids: Discovery House, 2006.

Bibliography

Swenson, Richard. *Margin: Restoring Emotional, Physical, Financial, and Time Reserves to Overloaded Lives.* Colorado Springs: NavPress, 2004.

Tedeschi, Richard G. and Lawrence G. Calhoun. "Posttraumatic Growth: Conceptual Foundations and Empirical Evidence." *Psychological Inquiry* 15, no. 1 (2004): 1-18.

Ten Boom, Corrie. *The Hiding Place.* 35th Anniversary Ed. With Elizabeth and John Sherrill. Grand Rapids, MI: Chosen Books, 2006.

The Blind Side. Directed by John Lee Hancock. 2009. Burbank, CA: Warner Bros., 2010. DVD.

The War Within: Finding Hope for Post-Traumatic Stress. 2010. Grand Rapids: Discovery House, 2010. DVD.

Tribus, Paul. *The Scars of War.* Seattle: WordSmith, 2005.

Vanauken, Sheldon. *A Severe Mercy.* New York: Bantam Books, 1977.

Vine, W. E. *An Expository Dictionary of New Testament Words With Their Precise Meanings for English Readers.* Old Tappan, NJ: Fleming H. Revell, 1966 First published 1940.

White, Jerry. *The Joseph Road: Choices That Determine Your Destiny.* Colorado Springs: NavPress, 2010.

Willey, Barry E. *Out of the Valley.* Ft. Worth, TX: Creative Team Publishing, 2016.

Yancey, Philip. *Where Is God When It Hurts?* Grand Rapids: Zondervan, 1977.

Young, Sarah. *Jesus Calling: Enjoying Peace in His Presence.* Nashville: Thomas Nelson, 2004.

APPENDIX 1
Products and Services

Books, Video Series, Training Game

RESILIENT WARRIORS
ISBN: 978-0-9838919-4-9

RESILIENT WARRIORS ADVANCED STUDY GUIDE
ISBN: 978-0-9838919-5-6

RESILIENT LEADERS
ISBN: 978-0-9855979-9-3

RESILIENT NATIONS
ISBN: 978-0-9897975-6-6

RESILIENCE GOD STYLE
ISBN: 978-0-9979519-2-9

RESILIENCE GOD STYLE STUDY GUIDE
ISBN: 978-0-9979519-3-6

RESILIENCE GOD STYLE VIDEO SERIES

RESILIENCE GOD STYLE TRAINING GAME

Appendix 1

Resilience God Style Video Series

- Includes powerful Biblical teaching
- Resilience stories designed for your small group
- Each Video is less than 30 minutes
- Parallels content in the Resilience God Style book and associated study guide
- Both virtual delivery and hard copy

The Resilience God Style Video Series addresses:
How do we prepare for the Storms of Life?
How do we weather these storms?
How do we bounce back without getting stuck in the toxic emotions of guilt, false guilt, anger, and bitterness?

VIDEO SERIES CONTENT
Includes GROUP LEADER INSTRUCTIONAL VIDEO
INTRO "Welcome to Resilience God Style"
LESSON 1 "We Will Have Tribulation!"
LESSON 2 "Better or Bitter?"
LESSON 3 "Resilience Life Cycle©"
LESSON 4 "BEFORE: The Ounce of Prevention"
LESSON 5 "DURING: Weathering the Storm"
LESSON 6 "AFTER: Looking Back"
LESSON 7 "AFTER: Pressing Forward"
LESSON 8 "Higher Than Ever Before!"

**ALL in the power of God
RESILIENCE GOD STYLE**
www.ResilienceGodStyle.com/Resources

Resilience God Style Training Game

- Comprehensive Interactive Learning System
- Fun way to learn critical resilience skills, based on Biblical principles.
- Creates a safe environment to discuss key life issues.
- Great team builder–for families, schools, churches, and organizations
- Complements Resilience God Style Book and Video Series.

Are you a tennis ball or an egg?
This training game
makes the difference
Resilience God Style!!!

www.ResilienceGodStyle.com/Resources
www.WinningTheTrainingGame.com

Appendix 1

FOR INFORMATION, COMMENTS, and QUESTIONS:

author@ResilienceTrilogy.com
administrator@ResilienceTrilogy.com
contact@ResilienceGodStyle.com

FOR SUPPORTING RESILIENCE CONTENT:

www.ResilienceGodStyle.com
See "Resources" tab for worksheets and presentations

Facebook: Resilience God Style

Twitter: @GodBounce

Instagram: ResilienceGodStyle

Resilience Consulting LLC
1801 Red Bud Lane
Suite B-298
Round Rock, Texas 78664

APPENDIX 2

Resilience Life Cycle© Summary Diagram

RESILIENCE LIFE CYCLE©

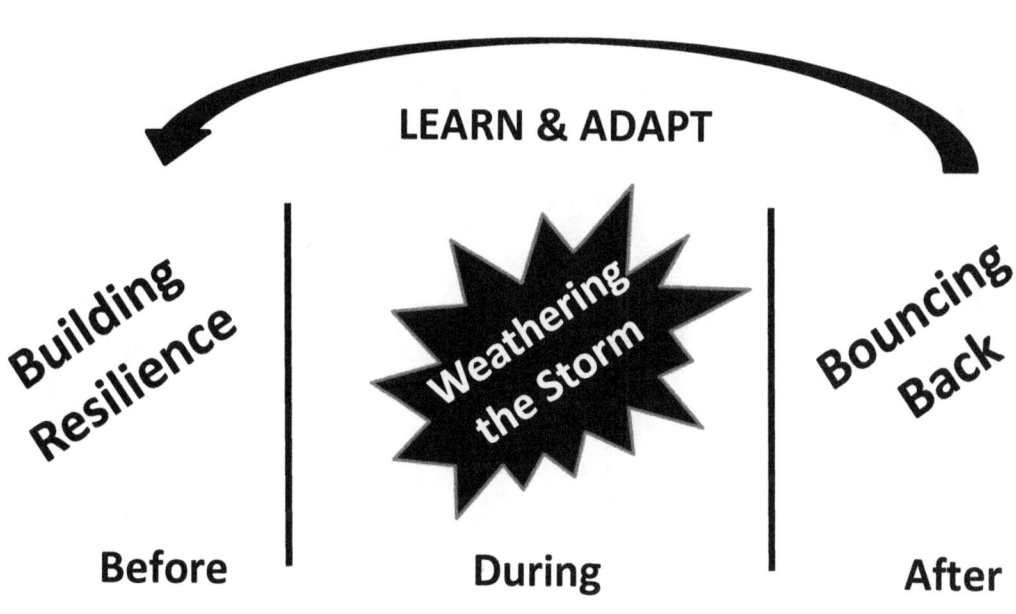

Before

- Know Your Calling (Mission, Purpose)
- Know Your Enemy
- Know Your Friends
- Know Your Equipment (Armor of God)
- Deploy with the Right Mindset
- Develop and Rehearse "Actions on Contact" (Get Ready!)

During

- Call 911 (Ask for help)
- Start the IV (Nurture yourself)
- Keep Breathing (Maintain routines)
- Draw from Your Well of Courage (Past strengths)
- Remember Your Calling

After

- Guard Your Primary Relationships
- Choose Forgiveness and Gratitude
- Grieve Well
- Sing a New Song
- Revalidate Your Calling (Discern and Chart the Future)
- Comfort Others

APPENDIX 3

Growth Through Adversity Tool

Growth Through Adversity: *A Critical Life Skill*

Analyze one of your life "body slams" in terms of the Resilience Life Cycle©

Resilience God Style, www.ResilienceGodStyle.com

1. **My "Body Slam:"** _____

2. **My Reactions:** _____

3. **My Thoughts:** _____

4. **My Feelings:** _____

Appendix 3: Growth Through Adversity Tool

RESILIENCE LIFE CYCLE©

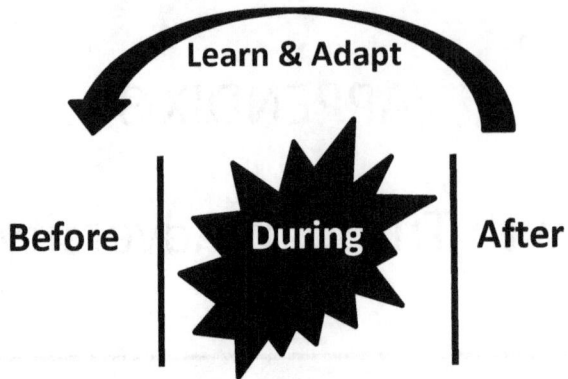

Resilience God Style, www.ResilienceGodStyle.com

BEFORE

1. Was I prepared for this life experience? _____
2. How could I "Get Ready" for this?
   A. _____
   B. _____
   C. _____
3. Did I have "Actions on Contact" prepared in advance? _____

DURING

1. How did I "Weather the Storm?"
   A. _____
   B. _____
   C. _____
2. What/Who were my "life preservers?"
   A. _____
   B. _____
   C. _____

AFTER

1. Did it get worse?
2. Did I grieve the loss? (D,A,B,D, Acceptance)
3. Did I get stuck?
   A. Guilt?
   B. Anger?
   C. Bitterness?
4. Am I still stuck?
5. How do I get unstuck?
   A. New Song?
   B. Forgiveness?
   C. Renewed Purpose?

LEARN & ADAPT

1. What did I LEARN?
   A. Before? _____
   B. During? _____
   C. After? _____
2. Did I GROW? How?
   A. _____
   B. _____
   C. _____
3. Did I ADAPT in order to "Be Ready" for future life traumas? _____

Reference: *Resilience God Style Study Guide,* pages 13, 14, 37-43

All Rights Reserved, Resilience Consulting LLC

APPENDIX 4

Fleeing a Spirit of Offense

"Therefore leaving the elementary teaching about the Christ, let us press on to maturity."
(Hebrews 6:1, NLB)

Why "fleeing?" My mind turns to the story of Joseph, when trapped and tempted by Potiphar's wife. It was not enough to politely say "No", nor was it sufficient to simply walk away. He had to flee, even without his garments, to break the enticement of that temptation. Or consider Lot's wife. While fleeing from Sodom & Gomorrah, she quit "fleeing" and looked back, an act of disobedience resulting in eternal condemnation as a pillar of salt. Hence, there are times when we should actively, aggressively, with all our might, flee temptation. As the scriptures admonish:

> *"...flee youthful lusts, flee idolatry, flee these things."—"But thou, O man of God, flee these things; and follow after righteousness, godliness, faith, love, patience, meekness." (I Timothy 6:11, KJV)*

Yes, we should flee those things that disturb our fellowship with God and with our fellow man. One of the subtle temptations we all face is to entertain a "Spirit of Offense." Although very subtle, such a mindset certainly disrupts personal peace and collective unity. Hence, this is a situation, an attitude, a mindset, a spirit we should flee from. First of all, what is a Spirit of Offense? How does it manifest itself?

- A Spirit of Offense is the opposite of a James 1:19, mindset: A Spirit of Offense is quick to speak (including rumors), slow to hear (including not hearing the positive aspects about others), and quick to become angry (or offended).
- Being "quick to take offense" often occurs
    - Without all the facts
    - On the word of a third party, or a rumor
    - On behalf of another who may not be offended at all

Appendix 4: Fleeing the Spirit of Offense

- Usually accompanied by rumors and "whisperings" (gossip)
    - *"What dainty morsels rumors are—but they sink deep into one's heart."* (Proverbs 18:8, NLB)
    - *"They visit me as if they are my friends, but all the while they gather gossip, and when they leave, they spread it everywhere." (Ps 41:6, NLB)*
    - *"Then when you call, the Lord will answer. 'Yes, I am here,' he will quickly reply. "Stop oppressing the helpless and stop making false accusations and spreading vicious rumors!"*
    - *"Do all things without murmuring and disputing, that you may become blameless and harmless, children of God without fault in the midst of a crooked and perverse generation, among whom you shine as lights in the world." (Philippians 2:14,15; NKJV)*
    - This makes for a very illuminating topic study. There are many more references which illumine God's thoughts about rumor, gossip, and "whisperings."
- Sometimes motivated by "selfish ambition and conceit:"
    - *"Let nothing be done through selfish ambition or conceit, but in lowliness of mind let each esteem others better than himself." (Phil 2: 3, NKJV)*

What are the results of such a Spirit of Offense?
- Disrupts unity, love, trust, and confidence
- Produces organizational and interpersonal tension, and "mini-crises"
- Saps energy, enthusiasm, and focus
- Undercuts established channels of communication and issue resolution

What are some ways to remedy a Spirit of Offense?
- Recognize that this is WAR. Satan prowls, seeking to devour. If he can't nail us on the big things, he'll try more subtle approaches. Hence, the Armor of God (Ephesians 6) is critical for protection and sensitivity to the subtle, but pernicious Spirit of Offense.
- A military maxim says "The first report is always wrong." Hence, don't jump to conclusions.
    - Develop heightened sensitivity to negative input about others...don't just accept at face value.
    - Assume the best about a brother or sister...grant a gracious "benefit of the doubt."
- Don't entertain or overly empathize with grievances expressed by another that should rightly be discussed in supervisory channels.

Appendix 4: Fleeing the Spirit of Offense

- Resolve interpersonal issues scripturally:
    - One on one
    - Then with an associate
    - Then formally within the organization.
- Exercise accountability regarding rumors and gossip. Work hard to keep oneself in check, and lovingly remind others as appropriate.
- Leadership makes a difference! Model a culture of grace and communication. Systemic information flow often eliminates the information vacuum in which rumors abound.
- As Paul exhorts in Philippians 4:8, *"Fix your thoughts (attitudes) on what is true and honorable and right. Think about things that are excellent and worthy of praise."* No doubt this also pertains to our words, as well as our responses to the words of others.

No doubt many reading this can add other rationale, and provide additional scriptural underpinnings. And… many model right behavior in this regard. **As a bottom line, however, I encourage you to join me in renewed efforts to personally flee from such a Spirit of Offense in our lives.** And may we together, as a team, rebuke this trick of Satan, as we proclaim the name of Jesus and as we walk in the power of the Holy Spirit. May God truly bless our application of these important truths as we seek to be *"doers of the word, and not hearers only, deceiving your own selves."*
(James 1:22, KJV)

Finally, *"Dear Brothers and Sisters, Be quick to listen, slow to speak, and slow to get angry."*
(James 1:19, NLB)

With Love and Great Respect,

Bob

Bob Dees

www.ingramcontent.com/pod-product-compliance
Lightning Source LLC
Chambersburg PA
CBHW060500010526
44118CB00018B/2483